Speaking in Tongues

THE BANFF CENTRE

PRESS

Published in association with PEN Canada

Library and Archives Canada Cataloguing in Publication

       Speaking in tongues: PEN Canada writers in exile / [edited by] Maggie Helwig.

ISBN 1-894773-17-9

       1. Exiles' writings. 2. Authors, Exiled—Literacy collections.
3. Literature, Modern—20th century. I. Helwig, Maggie, 1961-

PN495.S62 2005   808.8'99206914   C2005-900436-3

Editing by Maggie Helwig, Rennay Maclean, and Jennifer Nault

Book design and cover photography by Vangool Design & Typography

Proofreading by Lesley Cameron

Printed and bound in Canada by Houghton Boston Printers, Saskatoon, Saskatchewan

- -

 Canada Council Conseil des Arts
for the Arts du Canada

 Alberta
Foundation
for the Arts

The Banff Centre Press gratefully acknowledges the support of the Canada Council for the Arts and the Alberta Foundation for the Arts for its support of our publishing program.

The Banff Centre
PRESS

Speaking in Tongues

PEN Canada Writers in Exile

EDITED BY
Maggie Helwig

INTRODUCTION BY
John Ralston Saul

Contents

Acknowledgements

Thank you to the PEN Canada members and friends who donated their time and skills to help with the editing of some of these essays: Karen Connelly (who worked with Senthil Ratnasabapathy), Margaret Christakos (Mehri Yalfani), Alan Cumyn (Stella Lee), Janice Kulyk Keefer (Andrea Hila), Fraser Sutherland (Fereshteh Molavi and Faruk Myrtaj), Elke Willmann, Dr. Stephen Ahern, and Ken Simons (Benjamín Santamaría Ochoa); to His Excellency John Ralston Saul for writing the introduction; to the members of the PEN Canada Writers in Exile Committee, and to the staff and former staff of PEN, especially Isobel Harry, Philip Adams, and Margaret Christakos.

Thanks as well to Jennifer Nault at the Banff Centre Press for all her work on this project, and to everyone at the Banff Centre for their support of PEN's writers in exile, with special thanks to Carol Holmes, Director, Writing and Publishing, and Linda Gaboriau, Director, Banff International Literary Translation Centre.

Maggie Helwig

Foreword

PEN Canada — a centre of International PEN, a writers' association founded in 1921 — works within Canada and internationally to promote freedom of expression and aid writers persecuted for the peaceful expression of their ideas. PEN's work for many years focused on writers imprisoned for their writing in countries around the world, as well as freedom of expression issues in Canada. In the late 1980s and early 1990s, however, PEN Canada began working with exiled writers, initially not as policy, but in response to events. Chinese poet Duo Duo found himself exiled in Toronto after the Tiananmen tragedy in 1989. Journalist Martha Kumsa arrived from Ethiopia in 1991, after a brutal nine years and eight months in jail. The Bosnian poet Goran Simic and his wife, translator Amela Simic, arrived in Canada in 1995 through the work of PEN; and, over the same years, PEN Canada became aware of other writers in exile who had arrived in Canada on their own, and were trying to re-establish themselves as writers in a new land and a new language.

To its credit, the government of Canada has offered citizenship and passports to these and other threatened writers when other countries would not. But PEN soon realized that this was only the beginning of an exiled writer's transition. Uprooted from their old intellectual community, their literary and academic contacts, and in most cases the language in which they have always worked, writers in exile find themselves isolated. They are often unable to publish in Canada, or can publish only with "ethnic" periodicals and publishing houses, leaving them cut off from the larger literary discourse of the country.

PEN Canada has worked to establish partnerships with universities and colleges to secure temporary placements for writers in exile. Massey

College has been tremendously supportive from the earliest stages, and more recently we have had successful partnerships with George Brown College, Trent University, and Acadia University, among others.

But more than anything else, what writers in exile want is to be read by Canadians, to find a voice and an audience, to be able to participate in the development of Canadian culture; and they face a series of enormous obstacles in this. It can all, perhaps, be summed up in the word "translation."

First, and most obviously, is the problem of translating a writer's language. Very few of the PEN writers in exile are native English speakers. Most have spent a lifetime acquiring a kind of hyper-fluency in their own language, refining their skills and knowledge, studying their own literary traditions, creating a unique voice. To translate a literary writer, in such a way that even a part of their achievement is communicated, requires far more than simply putting the literal meaning of their words into English. Good literary translators are rare, and most of them work in a few major world languages. And for a writer to master English, in adulthood, to the level necessary to write serious literary prose or poetry, is a huge task, far beyond the scope of an ESL course. Over and over, when we talked to writers in exile about their problems, the difficulty of having their work translated came up as their greatest problem.

But there is more to be translated than language alone. Writers in exile arrive in Canada knowing no one from the literary community, in most cases; and almost always they find that, no matter how extensive their previous history, it does not "translate" to Canada. Writers with a dozen published books may find themselves starting over again from scratch, as if they were at the very beginning of their careers. And, all too often, their experiences and their cultural frameworks are unfamiliar to Canadian editors, who may need translation not only of the language, but of the material itself.

A writer writes because he or she must; and a writer writes to be heard. Whenever I have talked to writers in exile, what they want most of all is to be heard, to be read, to be appreciated, not only in their own ethnic communities, but in the wider Canadian discussion. This anthology is one attempt to break down the walls that stand between many of these writers and a Canadian audience.

The issue of linguistic translation came up, of course, as soon as the idea for an anthology was conceived. I myself am fluent only in English.

There was no possibility even of finding, much less of paying, literary translators in all the languages spoken by our writers. So a decision was made that all pieces would have to be written in English, though some of the writers are still learning the language. Each piece would then be intensively edited by another writer who was a native speaker of English.

This process has worked differently for each writer. A few already have a high degree of fluency in English, and required no more editing than any English-speaking writer would; others needed something close to "translation" to get their work into English in the way that they wanted. Some of the writers met with their editor/translator, others worked by e-mail; sometimes careful discussion was required even of individual words, to ensure that the writer's meaning and nuances were preserved as far as possible, while making the pieces understandable to an English-speaking audience. I edited about half the essays myself; the rest were edited by volunteers, mostly PEN members, all of them professional writers or editors.

While we were thinking about how to make this process work, it occurred to me that perhaps translation should be not only the central dilemma that the book faced in its preparation, but also the overarching theme of the essays. As Saghi Ghahraman, an Iranian poet in exile, put it in our discussions, "Translating the self into another self through another vocabulary is what we face, after we have made the crossing safely. It is the last border, and it is invisible, and it is there during the translation period that we slip away." I had recently written a novel that dealt in part with the problems of translation, and over more than a year of research had become interested in the ways that linguistic translation leads into larger questions of how we use language, and how we understand ourselves and the world. So, along with the Banff Centre Press, and mindful of the work of the Banff International Literary Translation Centre, we made the decision that this should be the theme we would ask all the writers to explore.

The result has been, I think, a fascinating collection of perspectives on translation. I was surprised, when the essays began coming in, to find that only a few of the writers had chosen to write about translation in the literal sense; those who have — for instance, Fereshteh Molavi and Faruk Myrtaj — are often themselves translators as well as writers. Many chose to write about the difficulty of "translating" their whole lives into the new context of exile in Canada, sometimes approaching the topic directly, like Stella Lee and Benjamín Santamaría Ochoa; sometimes, like Andrea Hila, more metaphorically.

Finally, some of the writers — Goran Simic, George Bwanika Seremba, Reza Baraheni — have taken on the concept of communication itself, the inherent ambiguities of translating experience into language. And it is here, perhaps, that the theme opens up to include all writers, indeed all of us who make our way through the world, reminding us that we are all in some way exiled from each other, none of us able to speak without translation, all searching for that language that will perfectly express us to each other.

Maggie Helwig

_ _ _ _ _

For more information about PEN Canada's work with writers in exile, writers in prison, and free expression in Canada and internationally, contact:

PEN Canada
24 Ryerson Ave, Suite 214
Toronto, ON, Canada, M5T 2P3
Tel: 416-703-8448
Fax: 416-703-3870
info@pencanada.ca
www.pencanada.ca

John Ralston Saul

Introduction

Writers must write. That's what they do. Writers who come to Canada in exile should not have to cease their craft. Living in Canada should not be an impediment to writers expressing themselves and earning their livelihood. In fact, we have a real obligation to try to help them have a life as a writer. One of the questions before us — and before the writers — is, what language shall they write in?

Some are lucky because their language is our language. They have been able to leave their country, establish themselves in Canada, and continue to write without a severe adaptation. One only has to think of the large number of Haitian writers who now live in Montreal and who continue to write in French or Creole.

But what of those whose language is neither French nor English? Are these writers to be forced to write only in Canada's official languages? In her essay, Fereshteh Molavi speaks at one point of the difficulty of working in a second language, which was for so long a *foreign* language, with the inherent distance and lack of understanding of the nuances. The diaspora of Canadian society is large enough that it should allow writers to continue to write in their native language if they so choose.

There are two points that must be made on the issue of language of publication. First of all, we must beware the false logic of "international languages." This simply recreates colonial patterns of the British or French empires. Second, to impose a second or a foreign language on writers cuts off their ability to express themselves fully, it confines their ideas.

I mentioned that we have an obligation to help writers earn a living. Obviously, this is difficult if we can't make their works available in the languages of Canada. So it is very likely that this obligation will involve a great deal of translation. Rather than seeing translation as an obstacle, I believe this could in fact be an opportunity for Canadian publishers and our literary community. Canada could easily become an international centre of publishing.

It wouldn't be much of a stretch, and there are examples of how it could be done in our recent past. One only has to think of the international community of Czech writers, which existed for years mostly through Toronto. Josef Skvorecky even won the Governor General's Literary Award for his book *The Engineer of Human Souls*. Originally written in Czech, this was the first fiction winner to have been written in a language other than French or English. Or think of Stefan G. Stefansson, the leading Icelandic poet for years, yet he lived on a ranch near Calgary.

Canadians too often defer international publishing to the Americans, the British, and the French. This puts us in a defensive mentality even when we are successful. Now is the time to act aggressively. To lead, not to follow. We have these writers coming to Canada, and several of them are being taken in by universities. It is easy to envision a collaboration between a number of publishers and the universities to share the costs and tasks of creating international collections.

Canada's cultural and intellectual institutions must help reflect the reality of our diaspora, of our world. Our free society allows these writers in exile the opportunity to express themselves in a way interesting to those outside our borders. We discover other cultures through foreign literature, but by reading exiled writers we may also discover truths about our own society. They introduce new concepts and new ideas about familiar things.

PEN centres are doing good things for exiles and that is as it should be. But this is not a paternalistic relationship. It is essential that those who are in exile become a voice for the Canadian public, for their homeland, for themselves.

His Excellency John Ralston Saul
January 2005

George Bwanika Seremba

An excerpt from
Napoleon of the Nile

- -

AUTHOR'S NOTE:

There are myriad ways of passing time. For a group of young Sudanese in Ethiopia, it's short, improvisational, innocuous skits. These short the-atrical excursions lead to an even longer journey for all of us to witness. The occasion is a special anniversary. Napoleon and his compatriots celebrate their arrival in yet another country of asylum. Their new home away from home.

Spewed out of Ethiopia by a military coup, the youthful refugees are subjected to a cruel and inhuman reception by the bureaucrats, the press, and the authorities. Behind "lock and key," their short theatrical skits acquire a different magnitude — a play — a vivid re-enactment of their initial exodus across the desert in search of a new home outside the Sudan eight years ago to the day.

On a makeshift stage in a Kenyan refugee camp, three people begin an arduous journey — over one thousand kilometres and close to ten months long. They are gunned and bombed by the government troops, the militia, and their very own people. Mother Nature herself conspires against them. The rhythm of life is one of drought and famine — set against a backdrop of unending civil war. Somehow life goes on, and the young man (Napoleon), a young widowed mother (Aluer), and the prover-bial Old Man, form a family — if not a trinity.

Ultimately Napoleon of the Nile *is a play about survival against all odds. The lucky few who manage to survive the exodus find that Africa's long unending nightmare does not end with the crossing of a border.*

*The play exploits Africa's myths, folklore, and legends as well as rit-
ual, song, and dance. Sometimes it makes surrealistic leaps into fantasy:
at times, its most eloquent statement is the sound of silence punctuated
by bombs and bullets.*

*(A gun goes off one more time as they exit, now crawling on their
bellies. Silence. Before the dust and smoke settle on the scene, the brigand
expressionless figure picks their blanket and tosses it off to stage right.
When the light comes up it's already morning. Aluer and Napoleon both
seem comparatively calm. One would think last night was no more than a
little "kerfuffle." Distant skirmishes can be heard.)*

NAPOLEON   I wonder what happened to the Old One?

ALUER   So do I .... He's safe enough I would imagine. Wherever he
is. It's a bit strange.

NAPOLEON   True. He probably went the other side of the guns.

ALUER   Then spent the whole morning looking for us.

(Slight pause.)

He probably dug a little hole last night and tucked himself in.
I wouldn't put it beyond him. Observing us escape and probably laughing saying: "I told you so, you pay an exorbitant
price only to be robbed by the very people you swore by."

NAPOLEON   At least they were kind enough to shoot over our heads.

ALUER   For what it's worth, yes.

NAPOLEON   They probably blew their cover. Now they are being
hunted and stalked by the government troops and the
militia.

ALUER   Those must be the skirmishes that started this morning. Can
you still hear them?

NAPOLEON   Yes. The more running battles they have the better. Maybe
one day soon we'll really laugh about it.

ALUER   God willing, why not? We must have been quite a sight.

NAPOLEON   Given the Old One a lot of food for laughter. If indeed he
did see us.

ALUER   Hand in hand. With me leading in front.

NAPOLEON   Then the back; depending on where the next gun to go off
            was.

ALUER   And all along saying in my mind: "God, if someone has to
            go let it be me, not Napoleon." If I must tell the Old One
            that I didn't wet my pants he will think I'm lying. My hus-
            band must be laughing too, God bless his soul. With tears in
            his eyes ... probably sulking like a baby, saying: "How come
            Napoleon is more protected than the U.S. President?"

NAPOLEON   They are like human shields aren't they?

ALUER   The Secret Service you mean. Trained to jump in between
            the bullet and the President.

NAPOLEON   What a job.

ALUER   Indeed. Can you imagine a husband or wife saying goodbye
            in the morning: "Don't worry my dear, I am insured for life"?
            and then it's hello Mr. President, if you ever get a chance to
            say a single word. All you do is worry about your job and the
            American people, who vote their President in and shoot them
            out of office, all in the name of democracy. Mr. President,
            I just want you to know that the bullet stops right here.

NAPOLEON   I think you should apply for the job, Mama Aluer.

ALUER   I know. Lots of food too at the banquets and the restau-
            rants.

NAPOLEON   Oh those, I hear there is a big one called McDonald's.

ALUER   Where did you hear about it?

NAPOLEON   At school. You should write to the President once we cross
            the border.

ALUER   It's still a long way. Besides I am not sure they accept black
            people.

NAPOLEON   To swallow the bullets or eat in the restaurants?

ALUER   I don't know, both.

NAPOLEON   Isn't America supposed to be a free country?

ALUER   I hear it depends who you talk to.

NAPOLEON   Harlem or Queens that's where most of our brothers and sisters live. You would probably stay at the Waldorf Astoria, just like the father in "Coming to America." You can meet Eddie Murphy, Arsenio Hall, and one day Michael Jackson the King of Pop himself.

ALUER   First I've got to get the job, Napoleon.

NAPOLEON   Write to the President.

ALUER   What about my son?

NAPOLEON   He will play basketball and become as good as Hakeem Olajuwon. We are Sudanese remember? Basketball is in our blood, it's our birthright.

    (The excitement is reaching fever pitch.)

ALUER   The desert brings out our indigenous ways of passing the time. My husband must be laughing at us wherever he is.

NAPOLEON   So would the Old One.

ALUER   He will probably catch us in the middle of the act.

NAPOLEON   This time he will just sit and watch the drama.

ALUER   Maybe seethe with rage and jealousy now that his pupils have come of age and usurped his mandate.

    (Inspired even more, Aluer steps out and starts dialling an imaginary telephone number on an old-fashioned phone.)

    Hello. Hello, is this the White House? Yes, I would like to speak to the President please.

NAPOLEON   What?

ALUER   The President of the United States of America.

NAPOLEON   *(Enjoying himself. Gets closer and "cautions" her.)*

    Be gentle. Nobody knows they are talking to a starved refugee that hasn't even come across the border yet.

ALUER   What do you mean I can't talk to him you ...

             (*Spits out the word.*)

             BUREAUCRAT. Do you know who you are talking to? Some
             of my ancestors came to your country in chains. Yes. Many
             unceremoniously buried like worthless cargo in a sea full of
             salt and sharks.

NAPOLEON   Calm down. Nobody likes to be shouted at, especially bu-
             reaucrats.

ALUER   Those that survived the back-breaking labour to build your
             country were each promised forty acres and a mule.

NAPOLEON   You are making them feel guilty now. They will accuse you
             of ... blackmail ... and nobody dialogues with terrorists, not
             until they become leaders.

             (*Insists into phone.*)

             Tell the president that we've always loved Republicans all
             the way back from Abraham Lincoln himself.

ALUER   His phone is ringing. He will be on in seconds.

NAPOLEON   Maybe he is asleep. Don't forget they are half a world
             away.

             (*Aluer is still "listening."*)

             He is probably napping.

ALUER   No, it's too early in the morning. We'll be lucky if he has fin-
             ished breakfast. What should I say, Napoleon? Mr. President
             Sir or simply Mr. President?

NAPOLEON   He is American. They are not terribly formal. I would just
             call him Mr. President. Don't forget to tell him you used to
             be an actor at Precious Blood.

             (*Aluer signals to him to be quiet.*)

ALUER   Hello. Hello Mr. President. Hi, my name is Aluer. Immaculate
             Aluer. I am a fellow thespian from the Sudan ... no ... not Fiji,
             the Sudan.

             (*Starts spelling it.*)

NAPOLEON   Louder. He is a bit … hard of hearing. There is some kind of gridlock, the senate is talking his ears off. Ask for his wife.

ALUER   Am I loud enough now?

(Pause. Spunky and gutsy.)

Oh well, it must be full moon. I'm sure your wife can understand that. She must have told you about the Farmer's Almanac and astrological calendars.

(Laughs.)

Anyway I am a young, prematurely widowed mother from Western Yiral, sorry Southern Sudan.

NAPOLEON   Get to the point.

ALUER   I am looking for a job in the secret service. Yes, as part of your entourage of human shields. I've worked as human fodder and indeed myself and a lot of my countrymen are mobile targets … as you probably know, there is no pay and no insurance but we do swallow bullets for a living.

(Pause. Napoleon is getting jealous. Aluer is listening to the President.)

NAPOLEON   *(On his knees, begging, holding onto Aluer's hand.)*

Don't forget me. I can always scrub the floors at Mcdonald's. Even Denny's for that matter. Beggars are not choosers and my knees are really supple. Please tell him I was a member of the school choir and I used to be an altar boy. I can scrub the floor until it turns into a mirror.

ALUER   Yes your excellency. No, no, no. I wish you could read my lips. I will not be a Welfare Queen. I also have a son and he is athletically brilliant. If he is well fed he will grow up to be the next Kareem Abdul-Jabbar.

(Pause.)

NAPOLEON   Has he hung up?

ALUER   No, he is talking to the First Lady.

NAPOLEON   It doesn't look good.

ALUER   I think the official who let me through is going to be fired.

NAPOLEON   You better tell him the truth before he hangs up on us.

ALUER   It doesn't look good ... I understand, Mr. President. We know how deeply you care ...That's right. We know how deeply you care for your own people. Nobody would like to see you tarnish the dream.

NAPOLEON   Here. Let me talk to him.

ALUER   To tell you the truth Mr. President we just love it here. Just one or two little things ... you remember that decree you signed? The one that outlawed the "Evil Empire"? Well we need a little help.

               (Pause.)

               I beg your pardon. Oh yes, the Queen.

NAPOLEON   The Queen? No, she's got her hands full.

ALUER   Who?

               (Quick whisper to Napoleon.)

               Mrs. Thatcher.

NAPOLEON   God no! Not her. We need a woman.

ALUER   It takes more than a skirt and a grocer's daughter to have the compassion of a true mother.

               (Now they both speak into the phone.)

NAPOLEON   All we want is for you to outlaw our country.

ALUER   Our government.

NAPOLEON   Tell them to start bombing in five minutes. Bomb the hell out of our government.

ALUER   Together with their running dogs.

NAPOLEON   All you have to do is tell them, Mr. President. Tell them you will bomb them until the "bloody" Nile changes its course. We've never doubted your humanity, Mr. President. All you have to do is say it. They will all pack up real quick and sprint to the North.

ALUER   With their tails hanging limply between their legs.

(They catch their breath, slight pause — burst into laughter.)

God! I'm glad nobody's listening.

NAPOLEON   Why?

ALUER   They would probably be wondering if we were crazy or not.

NAPOLEON   *(Laughs.)*

I remember someone cautioning me to keep away from someone because their eccentricities would rub off on me.

ALUER   *(More laughter.)*

I know, I should also have told you that if the Old One was eccentric, I myself was already fully certified in the eyes of most people.

NAPOLEON   Don't say that.

ALUER   Better this than sleepwalking.

NAPOLEON   *(Hurt.)*

It's not out of choice. Just like my snoring.

ALUER   True. Blessed are those, in fact, who can still afford to dream and snore ... when their own country is a nightmare.

NAPOLEON   With no end in sight.

ALUER   We've got to keep hope alive though.

NAPOLEON   Then we should make more little plays.

ALUER   I know. My cynicism hasn't helped.

NAPOLEON   Are you sure we spoke to the right President?

ALUER   It doesn't matter. They are all the same.

Andrea Hila

Lemon Tree

Many years ago I believed that confinement, like darkness, could protect us from the menacing world outside. I believed that, from the day I was born, my life had unfolded in different circles of a mysterious confinement. High walls, vaguely looming, followed my every step, whether I was going to school or church or coming back home. School, church, home — all of these places were walled in. Under the Ottoman Empire, churches in my country had to be built in the hidden parts of cities, camouflaged by walls and houses. High walls surrounded our homes as well; during the communist era, the experience of confinement kept growing, while our human dimensions shrank correspondingly. This geo-cultural phenomenon compelled us to find underground ways of living, in which imagination and reality coexisted. Within this confinement, our prayers were nourished by masterpieces of religious art: murals and carved wooden crosses. Inside our courtyards, on the other hand, we often drew pictures of flowers and trees — my favourite tree was always the lemon tree. And though we were able to communicate fluidly from one world to another, there was always the risk that we might lose one or both of these circles that were so necessary to our survival. The equilibrium of this mode of confinement was subject to the power of others: to lose something meant to confine you; something you also used as a hidden protector could lead to a double loss. This essay explores what lay inside — and what was lost outside — those confining, protective circles.

- - - - -

One-hundred square metres overall, the domain extended from our courtyard wall, back in Albania, to the high wall of the Franciscan monastery. A covert lemon tree and our hidden church: these real objects, which for me were also symbols, seemed to be strangely related to each other. As symbols they helped me to convey messages; as images they helped me to shape a virtual world. What I've come to realize now, after so many years, is that the life I lived in Albania — an unimaginably difficult time, with all possible privations — never prevented me from elaborating my confinement, even from a hallucinatory mise en scène, both physical and intellectual. It seems illogical, but under a brutal regime, which aimed to restrict our knowledge to what we must not do, I was still able to build up my small, secret kingdom, with mixed elements from both worlds, in full isolation from the outside world.

Our house and yard were surrounded by a high stone wall: an opaque aquarium in which humans, pets, and trees lived together. For contrast, there was the empty church nearby, where people in black lived buried behind high walls: two external circles of Dante's inferno with particles of heaven inside. The church's emptiness would fill with prayers, candles, and faith during secret ceremonies held in our houses. These things had to remain deep inside of us, regardless of what happened outside. Objects such as Easter eggs, these fertile symbols, played an enormous part in allowing us to stay true to, and to trust in, our beliefs.

That you can be confined by things that you trust may be the most difficult thing to understand about my earlier life. Solitary confinement provided our only way to perceive — as opposed to speak out about — the things making up our world. Sometimes in school, children would mistakenly confide their dreams to their teachers or even their friends. Our parents were afraid that their children might say things, however sincere, that could jeopardize the whole family. "Even walls have ears," they told us in hushed voices — an everlasting warning.

The lemon tree became to me an aesthetic symbol that stood for beauty and unrealized things. How so? Do children have aesthetic dreams? I think they do, for I imagined our old city as full of lemon trees. Not only its streets, but also along the lake shore: I imagined them growing right up to the old castle and finally becoming yellow clouds. In this way, all the children in our city could have lemons: the rain would fill their stomachs.

I even dreamed that the church itself — its murals, paintings, believers, wooden benches, and the soutanes of the priest — might have been yellow-green like the lemon. I felt the silence that veiled this yellow background with mystery, the mystery of people who silently record the murder of priests, silently fix in their memory the desecration of the sanctity of the church, whole generations of injustices. The colour of the blossoming lemon seemed to me like the song of a prisoner forced to sing loudly while others were being tortured to death. On the other hand, the silence of our church taught us how to feel without speaking, to confine the pain.

I never thought that this symbolism and its very complicated visual penetration of both my unconscious and conscious being would be revived right here in Canada. It did not return as a bad dream, but rather as a witness, wanting to express its own experience. This was the first exciting fruit that came from writing an essay about my experience. I discovered the second fruit during a party at the end of an English language course.

While celebrating the end of this course at our teacher's house, I began experiencing virtually the same feelings, with the same intensity and aesthetic greed, as I had back in my own country vis-à-vis the lemon tree. We were sitting in the backyard, its abundant grass and trees confined by a wooden fence. There were some plastic chairs and a table. The students were talking about matters such as how to obtain ESL teaching certificates, how to apply to universities, and employment opportunities. Meanwhile, my teacher and I were discussing some of my particular ideas about life; she said that she knew some people who would be interested in meeting me.

I turned our talk to the features of her backyard, especially the fence on both sides, a fence made of wood, one metre high, that let her see the houses of her neighbours. It struck me because even though some of the flowers in her garden were the same as those back in my country, such as roses, lilies, peonies, even forget-me-nots, there was a dramatic difference. For the beauty of backyards in Albania remained confined, like the beauty of the girls from our remote villages who displayed their flourishing youth only inside their houses. While this beauty, here, was ... naked. Sometimes, perhaps, you might have seen those girls from a distance on the back of horses, riding off to their unknown husbands. They were always circled, confined by dense crowds of people and horses. These concentric circles always cut off perception, creating absolute confinement.

I was asking myself, as we talked, if stone walls could make such a difference, securing our isolation as they did; I was interested in hearing from my teacher about her small fence, beyond which she could look directly at the faces of her neighbours. And all this time the view and the calm and friendly discussion were reminding me of my old backyard — the tree and the church that had nourished my childhood. For a good part of my life the lemon tree and the Franciscan monastery had silently fed me, and although the fruits of both symbols took time to come into their own, in my imagination they had long been flourishing.

What I didn't tell my teacher, but what I was thinking of the whole time, was the story of these two symbols.

— — — — —

For many years I had to get used to seeing our churches used as movie theatres or even sport centres, where people mocked priests and religion. In remote areas it was worse, with churches converted into depots. It was always difficult to get used to that transformation, to experience how a priest, a noble figure in our literature, could become a forbidden figure in our textbooks. It was difficult to know that in the same church where we used to pray, people were assembling to watch movies about Lenin — they had vandalized all of the artworks, masterpieces made by well-known painters, just as they had burned invaluable books. Strangely, when I compare both empires, Ottoman and communist, the second one seems more brutal. I remember, among many things, that when I wanted to baptize my first son, I had to go late at night, in secret, to ask our priest to come to our home. He had just been released from prison, where he had spent almost thirty years — held for no reason.

Could anybody have imagined that these half-empty buildings, used as depots for mere ideological purposes — though believers passing by would stealthily make the sign of the cross — would one day be returned to their former beauty? That the ancient libraries would reappear, along with schools and classes for children, and even the famous bells, now ringing joyfully? Could anybody have imagined that the remaining priests (and new ones) would be free to walk along the streets and be allowed to serve holy Mass to thirsty believers? These things actually happened in my country, where my grandparents had once been forced to hide their rosaries under their mattresses and to pray late at night so that observant children could not speak about these forbidden things to the neighbours. I still remember the pale colours of Mary and Jesus during the dark nights. The vivid imploring look of them, with rosaries in hands, like bare tree limbs standing stoically in a reddish dawn.

_ _ _ _ _

The history of my lemon tree is of interest not only because of how the tree miraculously started to bear fruit after so many barren years, but also because of how it foretold dramatic changes in our family. It is difficult to imagine how a lemon tree, planted for decorative purposes at the edge of a courtyard wall (during cold winters we longed to have a green tree that would bear fruit out of season), became an oracle of family events. During the long, difficult years when it refused to produce a single lemon, we used to gaze sorrowfully at its limbs empty of flowers, its trunk growing so fruitlessly. At that time, lemons were rarities: only a few families had lemon trees, most of which were planted in vases inside the house. The fruit was expensive, used mostly as a popular remedy for sore throats. For almost thirty years our lemon tree continued to be sterile, even after my father had someone graft limbs onto it from a fruit-bearing tree. Nevertheless, its full leaves looked friendly; during cold winters they gave us a sense of warmth that seemed to penetrate through our closed windows.

Just as we became free to go to church and attend holy Mass, the story of the lemon tree took a sudden, startling turn; one day, instead of seeing just leaves and a few flowers (which fell days after their first appearance), we found fruit actually growing from the branches. In the first year the tree produced only four lemons, in the second year the number doubled, then every year that followed more and more fruits appeared — all big and healthy. In those days, I would sit down on the outer ladder of my house. "These fruits are big," I'd think, "bigger than I have ever seen. What a blessing that I fed myself as I did." It seemed a good omen, even though I was not superstitious and did not yet know how events in my life would unfold.

The lemon tree began to increase its yield and size of fruit dramatically; after three years, it was full of big and splendid fruits, as in a painting of Van Gogh. Not without wonder, I saw that just like the lemons, items of good news kept coming up one by one during this long

period of time. Most importantly, my career began to flourish with the
same intensity as the lemon tree. First I got a job as a journalist with a
prestigious international radio broadcaster; then I published my short
stories books, winning a national prize, scholarships abroad, and travel
to Germany. I undertook humanitarian work, and ended by coming to
Canada: these have been some of the fruits of my career. "The lemon
tree has gained a moral status and become the symbol of our family's
prosperity," I would say, flattering its fertility. Only my mother seemed a
little sad, spending more time in the backyard taking care of the flowers
and, especially, the lemon tree.

This symbiotic trajectory continued for several years until I decided I needed to leave Albania. After that, something untoward happened to our mystical lemon tree. One day, the weather became cool,
signalling that it was time to take measures to protect the more delicate
trees. Already the sun was shining from a greater distance. And then, on
one of those rare nights that always seem to bring something new with
their suddenness, it snowed so heavily that everything turned white.
My mother, alarmed, went out to care for the lemon tree. She knew its
limbs should be shaken right away to free them from this heavy weight.
"Please," I said, "wait until tomorrow. I have to take some pictures of the
tree." I knew that it was risky to leave the lemon tree covered with snow,
but its beauty was irresistible. And indeed, I never took more striking
pictures than on that night: a dark aura surrounded the lemon tree,
which was covered in snow, enormous pieces of yellow fruit appearing
within its hidden limbs. Suddenly, I became aware of the risk I had taken
just for an instant of aesthetic satisfaction. In the future, I would risk
much more than that. I would lose my symbols one by one as I set out
on my adventures — but in exchange for what?

The next day was wonderful, the sun shining, children playing,
the sky an amicable blue, and the sun falling gently and touching all of
the trees — except my lemon tree. I noticed that its leaves were changing. Their colour was that of a person's eyes upon their last breath: the
shine had withered. The leaves hung lifeless, while the skin of the trunk
seemed worn out. We all stood without talking for a long time in front of
the tree, a sadness veiling the house. I still remember the distant look in
my mother's eyes, tinged with sadness. Was the lemon tree experiencing
our decision to leave as a tremendous loss? Who knows? We all knew
we would bury something here with each departure.

After a few days, we made another risky decision: my wife and children and I finally left our country for Canada. My sister followed. We often telephone my mother. She is beginning to feel better; her pain at our absence seems to be diminishing, but we all know that things will never be as they once were. The tone of my mother's voice changes to pleasure when she hears about my children's experiences at school or our progress in the same fields of work we pursued in Albania. When I speak to her, she tells me about the old lemon tree. She told me that some small new buds have begun to show up. I still don't know if I should believe her or not; I will have to wait until I return one day to my old, abandoned backyard.

Meanwhile, here in Toronto, just as in Albania, my wife takes care of the flowers, setting them in vases close to the window. Sometimes we go to church, but it's different somehow. We miss our lemon tree, our confinement, while we are still getting used to new conditions. Yet I like to contemplate the symbolism of the lemon tree as a perennial phenomenon. Once more, I have begun to experience a trace of the old perception, that of being surrounded by known things: grass, and the limbs of trees, that go far beyond the limits of a courtyard. At that end-of-class celebration, when my teacher finished her description of her backyard and her neighbours, I spoke up. I told my teacher that courtyards differ; ours were made of stones and were high enough to hide us from the eyes of neighbours. Sometimes, though, the rough stones would also hide all too well the intimacy and the charm of lovely things. "I would like that kind of isolation," she replied, adding that she, too, longed for a little privacy.

It was quiet; her son was lying on the grass, and nobody seemed to be around in the other backyards, which looked like small parcels viewed by all. And in that quiet, a question echoed in my ears — it still echoes today. What else did I put at risk in the long, long journey to Canada?

Zdenka Acin

Lost and Found in Translation

My existence is a paradoxical one. Canada is the country I've chosen. I was not born in Canada, but I am a Canadian by my own decision, my own free will and choice. At the same time, Canada is the country of my exile. However, that situation is probably more natural than the one I had before. I was born in the Balkans but there, in my former homeland, as a dissident and non-fiction writer, I was also in exile. It seems that anywhere I go I am a stranger; both in this part of the world (which I have chosen) and that part (over which I did not have a choice).

Anyhow, an airline *translated* me from Belgrade and Budapest into Toronto. One could say I practically fell from the sky down here. "To fall from the sky" means that you have been *translated* from nowhere to nowhere. Somehow it reminds me of the challenge that Arseniy Tarkovsky (father of the famous Soviet filmmaker Andrei Tarkovsky) had to deal with when one night he received an order to translate Joseph Stalin's poems from Georgian into Russian. Tarkovsky, a noted poet and a respectable translator of Asian languages, had a choice: either translate the contents of the poems whilst paying no attention to rhymes or take care of the form and thus neglect the contents. In both cases he would betray the original and the punishment would be death. Any text that has to be translated under strict conditions imposed by some absolute, ideal translation is text no more. It is a no-text. Translating no-text can only be no-translating. My existence is just like that: no-translating of a no-text.

So, what does translation mean to me? I talk about it with my friend Michael Scammell, one of the best translators from Russian into

English, and he told me that the impetus to translate works from other languages is fundamentally emotional and derives from two main sources. The first is the discovery in another language of works of great literary and aesthetic value that impress (or even overwhelm) one with their beauty and meaning. The second is an urgent desire to communicate one's experience to other readers (in this case, readers of one's own language) who cannot read the works in question in the original language. It is an act of altruism and generosity that also fulfils a kind of pedagogical urge, which says: "Look at this. This is terrific. You ought to know about it and you will enjoy experiencing it."

I could say I agree with Scammell's opinion. However, if translating is seen as a kind of *survival*, I remain without beauty and meaning. I am translated, but meaningless. I see myself more and more as unfaithful translation. It is absolutely clear to me what it means when we say that translation is always a betrayal. My existential language as the exile's language is full of foggy expressions — foggy, but not always black. In other words, there are still some chances left for translation.

Welcome to the world of translation!

I will take you now to the world of the subway.

Metaphorically speaking, the world of the subway is a great stage on which we are all principal actors (those who are louder than others in their "roles") and background performers (silent actors who add verity to the main action). At the same time, we are all spectators and above all — *translators*.

The Toronto subway is the stage of mini-mankind, since in one single compartment one can see people from all around the world. Almost reminiscent of the biblical passages in which all languages are mixed, the confusion of tongues after punishment for the Tower of Babel. Here, no monoglot could understand anyone outside his own language. Only those polyglots who speak English — as the official language in this country — could secure understanding of each other.

The other day, I witnessed a subway play. Its cast included (as principal actors) a woman and her two small daughters (one girl around five years old was sitting next to her mom, but another, maybe around eighteen months old, was sitting in her stroller in front of her sister and mom). They were speaking in French with a *lady* who had in her hands some kind of women's magazine. While they were talking, she was showing some pictures from the pages to the small girl in the stroller.

Another principal actress was a young woman, who was sitting just across from them holding her one-year-old girl who was in the "role" of crying. Finally, part of the cast was a young couple standing in the middle of this scene, talking — I assumed, since I couldn't hear properly — about some traditional Italian dish that was resting in a cardboard box that the young man was holding in his left hand.

When I entered the stage, the only seat I could take was the one across from the French family, next to the young woman who was holding her small crying girl. My attempt to attract the crying girl's attention and rescue her from her tears was unsuccessful but I was surprised that even her mother didn't react to my simple, friendly question, "What's wrong, baby?" That is the question to which moms usually react by explaining that their child is sleepy or tired or frustrated for this or that reason.

Not this mom.

She didn't even react when the small girl from the stroller began to point out at her daughter, "Baby, baby!" endlessly repeating it while her forefinger was curiously extended towards the girl (still restless in her mom's arms), stopping briefly between some, I assume, frustrated requests which I didn't understand. It was obvious to me, however, that the stroller-sitting girl wanted contact with "the baby."

Suddenly, while at Rosedale subway station — which is a section of the route where the train runs above ground — the cellphone of the woman sitting next to me started to ring. I overheard some Arabic language. It may have been Syrian but I couldn't be sure.

The baby was quiet for a moment. However, the lady with the magazine couldn't keep the attention of the girl in the stroller, no matter what she showed her — having teased her previously as to whether she liked the picture of nicely decorated food more than the picture of the nicely decorated house. Being a good eater (it was pretty visible on her rounded face), the small girl had previously always chosen pictures with food and that caused the lady and girl's mom to laugh and make some comments I couldn't understand (clearly due to my poor French). I could only assume that they were commenting on the girl's good appetite. None of them paid any attention to the oldest girl in this small subway kindergarten.

However, I was her spectator, and she performed for me a "telephone" conversation by putting her mom's pager to her ear. I couldn't hear any single word of that imagined phone conversation but I was really very curious to whom she was "talking." "What language?" I wondered to myself, yet I was once again attracted by the performance of the small girl in the stroller who was very eager to be involved in communication with the "baby" who was crying again. Her attempt was so funny to me that I made a comment — talking more to myself than to the girl — since I had realized that she also spoke only French. I said, "But what are you then if she is a baby?", because for me she was a baby, too. Alas, I didn't expect that I would be heard by the young couple holding the traditional Italian dish, who were sitting now on the seats aside, facing me, and our intercommunication was established by friendly laughter. Finally, I thought, someone in this "play" understands English, which is my second language, but no word was spoken yet between us.

Out of the blue, both girls — the one in the stroller and the one in her mom's arms — began laughing loudly. They became locked in a competition as to who could laugh louder and longer. They didn't say a single word to each other. Even if they had, none of them would have understood what was said. I am almost sure that they knew it subconsciously but they communicated quite extensively (from all appearances) through their laughter. The two of them would periodically glance at me from time to time and I was also laughing, but not as loud ....

Looking at the laughing and now very happy baby, I realized that our language barrier was the reason why I couldn't catch her attention while she was crying. She simply did not understand the English language.

Then I made eye contact with the young couple while we were smiling at this performance of the youngest actors on the underground train and I said, "They don't need to speak the same language to understand each other. They don't need translation for their laugh. They both speak a universal language — language that doesn't require translation in their innocent world of the pure and metaphysical language of laughter." My fellow travellers nodded their heads in a motion of agreement.

All in all, during this entire underground pantomimic play, no words were exchanged between the woman sitting next to me, the French women and their children either, and very few between me — a woman with Serbo-Croatian as her first language and who speaks English — and lovers of traditional Italian cuisine who also speak English, though their first language could be Italian. But at the end of the scene we communicated through our unspoken but universal language which didn't need to be translated as it was the language of laughter.

Could we call it transcultural or intercultural communication?

But children can laugh. Can't they?

The subway is theatre but "the play" is universal. As long as the universal play exists, everything has not yet been lost. Nothing remains untranslated because every original is at the same time its own translation, a perfect translation. In this translation I have found myself together with my "errors" and existential paradoxes.

My friend Scammell reminds me that it often comes down to a struggle between being too faithful to the original language (in other words too "literal") and straying too far from the original in order to be idiomatic in one's own language. There is also the question of how to interpret what you are translating, and here Scammell gives me a personal example. Many years ago, he was translating Dostoevsky's *Crime and Punishment* into English and noticed that because of the speed at which the Russian novelist wrote, many of his sentences were awkward or ungrammatical. Scammell's tendency was to "correct" them or tidy them up in English, which is what most translators do. But then my friend had a brilliant professor of Russian literature at Columbia, also a specialist on Dostoevsky, who pointed out that part of the psychological discomfort the reader feels when reading Dostoevsky in the original stems precisely from these awkward or ungrammatical sentences which contribute to the oppressive atmosphere of the novel as a whole. Accordingly, Scammell changed his approach and incorporated these blemishes into his translation.

In my migration from one world to another, from one language to another, I must also admit my "errors" and blemishes. That is the art of translation. That is also the art of survival. That is the art of losing and finding ourselves in translation. Then I can laugh, can't I? Although it is true that I am not sure I can do it forever!

Well, I am a philosophical and literary translator. As Verba Volant Volunteer for the Logos Group in Italy, I daily translate one sentence by some famous author — philosopher, writer, actor, politician, historian, movie director, etc — and one word from English into Serbian. However, the whole paradox of my intellectual position came to light when one of my essays, written originally in English for a PEN reading on the Day of Imprisoned Writers, was translated from English into Serbian, without even my prior knowledge!

To explain what translation means for me philosophically, I'll again use the words of Michael Scammell, who thinks that this is a question that incorporates social, political, and cultural issues in one bundle. In essence, states Scammell, translation has been absolutely crucial to the world's development since the beginning of time. Taking our own Western tradition into account — the whole of our culture over the past two thousand years has rested on translations of the Bible and of the Greek and Roman classics. Without translations we (in Scammel's interpretation meaning Western civilization) would have had no literature, no science, no politics, no art, no culture ... nothing of any intellectual or philosophical value. And without translations we would have had no access to the intellectual and cultural riches and accomplishments of the Arabic world, the Chinese world, or the cultures of dozens of other nations throughout history.

But how do you take statements in one language with its own particular grammar, syntax, vocabulary, and cultural, philosophical, and ethical outlook and transpose it into another language with a different set of symbols, conventions, and meanings? One answer, Scammell admits, is simply that "you don't!" Translation is always a betrayal. "Traduttore —traditore," say the Italians — to translate is to betray — and in a literal sense it's true, for it is literally impossible to say exactly the same thing with exactly the same implications and meaning in two different languages. This points to the solution, which is, according to Scammell, always a compromise, a finding of a sort of middle ground that captures as much as possible of the meaning of the original without betraying (there's that word again) the character and spirit of the receiving language. But these point back to the philosophical question again, attesting that languages and cultures grow through being pummelled and stretched to accommodate new concepts, new meanings — and even new objects.

And finally, what about the literary aspect of translating? Scammell thinks that some of the same dynamics apply as in the linguistic field. The translation of works of literature from another language and culture often requires adjustment to different concepts of genre or the invention of a new genre to express the true qualities of the original work. Similarly, it is impossible to capture all the implications and nuances of meaning in the original so that again the translator is faced with the need to compromise. Whatever happens, the translator is forced to choose and that is why two translations of the same original can be so unalike (it's also why multiple translations of classic works continue to be worked and reworked). Each generation seems to need its own interpretation of the original in a contemporary language. But it's also a question of taste and of the taste or even bias of the translators themselves. Scammell's own preferred metaphor for this activity is the musical one. A translator "plays" a text the way a musician plays a score. The text is immutable, but the number of different possible interpretations is infinite, and each translator will choose a different way to play.

Could we then negotiate translation? Umberto Eco thinks we could.

How could we negotiate irony, sarcasm, cynicism?

In the innocent world of a child's laughter there is no such negotiation. They simply laugh.

We all have to learn how to laugh so we can better understand each other, no matter where we are translated. In finding ourselves in translation, we will find others. In the understanding of ourselves, we will understand others. Others are not a hell, but a new book to be translated.

So I am too.

I am the book waiting to be translated. I am a score longing to be interpreted in a faithful way. Without betrayal, please!

And then I will have to write a new essay in order to reconsider everything that was said in this one on the account of faithfulness and betrayal in translation, and what was lost and found in translation ...

Nevertheless, I am a book and a score, waiting not only to be translated and interpreted, but to be read, heard, and understood.

Fereshteh Molavi

English Has *Raped* Me

- -

Today exile and emigration, as global phenomena, have afflicted Iran, too. Yet in the past, facing invasions from Arabs, Mongols, and Turks, Iranians were reluctant to leave their land and generally preferred to tolerate, or compromise with, foreign or local tyrants rather than flee. To explore and examine the issue of immigration in its widest sense, embracing exiles and refugees, is too dense a topic for a short essay. However, I must point out that the waves of Iranian immigration during the past twenty-five years, the consequence of an authoritarian religious regime, is part of an overwhelming global movement closely associated with other general features of our age, and globalization in particular. Deriving from the problems of immigration, this essay also derives from a particular perspective and from a personal history.

English has *raped* me! One significant proof of this claim is that the very word *rape* so dominates my mind. Nonetheless, I do not mean to declare and prove a crime, but to report an event. I say it again: "English has *raped* me!" I never thought that one day I would use the first person singular pronoun as the object of such a sordid verb. Not because I assumed that rape was impossible, but because I greatly feared it. The fear of rape, even when not acknowledged, remains in women's minds, hidden but always present. Rape has a particular quality of violence. Nowadays, violence does not seem as indecent as it did in the past because the media constantly displays a wide range of physical and mental tortures. Yet, not only in traditional closed societies but also in the West, rape connotes the utmost in torture. This might be considered an outcome of a still-dominant patriarchy.

Patriarchy views women and their chastity as a precious property possessed exclusively by men, and thus its plunder is especially heinous. I recall nights in Tehran in the 1960s when any steps behind me caused fright as I walked between bus stop and home on my way back from an evening English class. I also recall the nights of Toronto in the late 1990s, fearful of rapists and serial killers on my route home from an evening computer class. Thanks to my innate talent for breaking clichés, I sometimes tried to think about a rapist as a victim and thus acquit him of the crime during this second period. Going further, I attributed my fears solely to patriarchal ethics and concluded that if such an incident occurred at the dark edge of a ravine, I should imagine that the cold ground was, say, an examining table in a gynecologist's office. On such nights, these naïve fantasies could more or less reduce my panic-stricken pulse and the toxic intensity of the moment. However, these imaginings could not reduce the overall ferocity of the fear nor, when all seemed safe, could reason or intellect diminish the threat. Though freed from traditional or patriarchal dogma, considering the rapist neither a victimizer nor a victim, as a woman, I still find rape hateful.

I've often thought that a brutal intrusion into a soul or mind — even more than into one's body, land, or property — would be impossible without consent. Reading the story of Faust, I concentrated on Faust's willingness to compromise with Satan and overestimated his compliance. This assumption pleased me because it summoned the belief that one could possess a soul or mind absolutely and safeguard it from any destructive invader. Should a writer cross a border, I thought, she would be secure in knowing that her wealth was safely within. When it was time for me to cross the border, my mind and language were wealth invisible to inspectors and worthless to customs officials. The sweet fantasy of bearing my home on my back forever like a snail crept into my mind. At that point, the idea didn't seem naïve. When the fundamentalist regime founded by the Ayatollah Khomeini crushed the opposition and many Iranians obsessed about exile, I thought my devotion to writing would prevent me from leaving my native land. After private, long-nurtured practice, I could see that my writing had improved and I felt that my relationship with language had advanced. At that time, I was unafraid of dangers or trouble waiting for me beyond my country's borders. My anger towards an authoritarian regime was so harsh that I did not dwell on what I might have to leave behind. The idea of leaving was clearly stronger and more reasonable than the idea of staying. Still, an inner voice told me otherwise. In the twenty years I remained in a place that was my language's home, I felt confident that my instinct was right. Regardless of the sufferings imposed on me in a land ruled by Islamic fundamentalists and all my inner despair, I stayed. Remaining there allowed me to plunge and immerse myself in the ocean of my first language — while not by choice, if I had been given a choice, it would be my ideal language. Over the years of internal exile in my disaster-stricken home, the Persian language (Farsi) was not only the light of my home, but my light *and* my home.

English has *raped* me! This statement is a confession rather than a complaint to the police. This is why it is so hard to say. Rape may be the crime about which victims are most reluctant to complain. Since its victims are mainly women, the fearful reluctance may derive from the prohibitions of patriarchal ethics. In a traditional society, within the domain of religious power, the pressure to conceal sins, as well as the willingness to observe taboos, is greater than it is in an open society. Regardless of what a society may impose on or expect of an individual, the physical conjunction between the criminal and the victim makes revelation difficult. While spiritual invasion is imposed on the victim, rape intrudes. The victim becomes implicated in a sin that has been initiated by another but committed inside herself. This may make the victim feel that she is an accomplice. Faust's covert/overt and voluntary/involuntary compromise with Satan comes to mind. Yet, before measuring what part rapist and victim each contribute to linguistic rape, we need to understand how it happens.

After leaving my fatherland, the home of my mother tongue, I might have arrived in a country where English wasn't spoken, but I didn't know what such a language would do with me or what I would do with it. Besides general features as a medium of communication, every language has a specific context and distinguishing characteristics. In the case of English, two factors had a significant role in what has happened to me. First, English is considered to be a global language by many people, and certainly it has a global *position*. Regardless of contradictions in the idea of "World English," or whether English speakers have the right to spread it all over the world, English is certainly the dominant language in science and technology as well as commerce and communication. Moreover, English has spread its influence over the world of the arts and literature. This position endows it with a power and ease of movement. Second, English is *my* first foreign language. A foreign language is obviously not the mother tongue learned in a mother environment and, outside its natural milieu, it is powerless to impose itself or to supplant the native language. For me, English lacked supernatural power. It appeared to me as my first foreign language when I was in Grade 7, and it was a window on the infinite perspective of world literature and science. Though I started learning it mainly at the British Council, I never found it invasive. As a "foreign language," it was a tool for accessing the most valuable human legacies: arts and science. It was also a means of communicating with other cultures. Thus, it was more than useful — so pleasant, so magnificent, in its right place, and it didn't interfere with my native language.

English also appears in another mode, as "English as a Second Language." This term, taken from comparing it with the "first language" (another name for mother tongue but disregarding its emotional aspects and only reflecting the language's rank) resonates as a survival language for immigrants living in an English-speaking country; it is a guarantee of their social-cultural presence in the new society. English is the most basic tool of communication with the host society and the only permit to be accepted by it. Whereas EFL does not delve into the culture of people whose native language is English, the basic function of ESL is for the learner to assimilate with this new culture. The deterministic force and covert compulsion of ESL give it an aggressive and dominating manner from which EFL is free. The difference between EFL and ESL results from their different roles: While EFL is aimed towards friendship and companionship, ESL imposes force.

Clearly, the "English" that has raped me is my subject, not the other English, whose company has always been delightful. In my view, the only position and function of ESL demands is forced intercourse. But why and how do I see this intercourse as forced? Involuntary emigration is the factor that makes the relationship with the second language undesired and coerced. Yet its force is indirect, and it is the immigrant who, for whatever reason or expectation, approaches it and places herself in its grasp. So the involvement is somewhat mutual, though the strength and intensity of one partner eclipses the other's role. When I state, "English has *raped* me," I do not mean to conceal my passivity or, for that matter, my actions. This is why I emphasize that I am not complaining of a crime but confessing an event. Yet this does not reduce the intensity, painfulness, and forcefulness of the event. Having intercourse with ESL, as in the case of a typical immigrant without any particular sensitivity to language in general, may stop at the stage of a long-term, difficult challenge — sometimes a debilitating one with a profound psychological impact and unforeseen consequences. Regarding my own personal devotion to Farsi, this interaction becomes an invasion of the privacy of a mind in love with a native language.

The claim that there is a conflict between second language and first language derives from a particular attitude towards language. One may say that language is a tool for communication. Or one may accept that language is a fundamental part of culture, even that it is the index of culture. From an extreme perspective, one could say that the mind depends on language. The difference between viewing language as a basis for the mind and language as a tool of social communication is significant. Likewise, language users vary in how they use the different aspects of language as well as how their minds consort with the layers of language. A love for a particular language is based on the understanding that mind and language are inseparable. In this case, the language user claims, "Language is what comes to me and stays with me; it is what comes inside me and comes out of me. Language is what happens to me and passes with me; it is what happens inside me and passes through me." Given this, a mind free of language, in a human context, is impossible. Further, a language free of the impact of complicated mental and emotional functions is hardly more than a set of limited codes unsuitable as anything more than a tool. From this perspective, language, first and foremost, reflects the inner self rather than the content of one's mind to someone else.

So, whatever happens in the mind of a single individual can only be reflected as a mirror, with language being the unique manifestation of a certain mind. This does not deny the presence of dreams and other non-verbal elements. However, anything in the unconscious, in order to make itself recognized by the mind, has to be manifested in the language of that mind. For example, a garden that suddenly appears in the dream cannot be recognized unless it receives the linguistic sign "garden." At the very moment it appears, it is labelled "garden." The more language users become aware of the presence and influence of language, the more the mind and language merge. In this case, the interaction between mind and language is subtler and more complex, for they both flourish side by side and each affects the other.

Occasionally, native English speakers discriminate against non-English-speaking immigrants. This, along with consequences of the global reach of English, gives English a dominating quality. Yet, from my perspective, the force of English deprives me of my privacy with my ideal language. In fact, English thrusts other languages into the remote part of non-English speakers' minds so forcefully that the fear of the death of "mother tongues," and particularly the fear of losing my own mother tongue, turns my dreams to nightmares and so I constantly hear the words, "English has *raped* me."

Yet this is not the whole story, for it lacks the last confessional installment. Having given English a human image, I have to endow it with duality and thus the dark and light sides of its face. In this way, English's identity is not divided into foreign language and second language. A language appears at the mental threshold with all its characteristics and looks for a way to enter. This language, regardless of its individual characteristics, shares general features with all languages. It conveys human things. I see a stranger at my door who desires to be known, who provokes in me a desire to know him — an unwanted guest asking to be admitted. This is a language wishing to be your friend. I am tempted to let it become one. Sometimes I catch myself enjoying English, without minding its foreignness, without being overwhelmed by its names and labels, and without being obsessed by my situation as an immigrant. In these moments, I naturally try not to think about the dark side and aggressive spirit of a violating stranger. Instead, I'd rather open my soul and mind to the smooth and inclusive flow of the language that approaches me. The joy of the intercourse between mind and the other language is momentary, though, since it does not lead to completion and ultimate pleasure. There is the unfamiliarity, for one thing; for another, the looming shadow of the first language.

The last instalment of my reluctant confession is only part of an overwhelming whole in my mind. To me, English is not a second language gradually forcing the first language back. Instead, it relies on and is supported by the characteristics of language; it draws attention to itself, attracts me, and fascinates me with its peculiar virtues. I return to the story of Dr. Faust and note that in his interaction with Satan, determinism and will are both involved, though they may be unequal.

While I was in love with my home, the circumstances appeared to me as in the image of Mephistopheles, revealing the magic power of English as the only code to my survival. In order to survive, I've grabbed the end of a rope and Satan is holding the other end. I've paid the price but, nevertheless, I've grabbed the rope to keep from falling. I do not pretend that I may be unable to protect the light of my home and the home of my light from time. Yes, English has raped me, yet ....

Benjamín Santamaría Ochoa

We, the invisibles

SHAME AND DISDAIN

Once upon a time I had a dream. The dream was that I was not dreaming.

Its image: I'm running naked at night, my newborn baby in my arms, through a gauntlet of soldiers on a narrow, cobbled street. The light rain turns from comforting to sinister. I arrive at a stadium, its green fields evenly lit by searchlights from above. There, another line of soldiers — generals this time — makes me feel ashamed of my nakedness and my fragile human form. I want to be invisible but can't. This recurrent dream chased me every day during the year I lived in Argentina, the last year of the military dictatorship.

Later, in my own country — after the murder of Digna Ochoa, when I, too, began receiving death threats — the sinister climate of my dreams turned into a daily presence. This is part of the story I want to tell to my street kids if I ever go back to Mexico.

It's winter in Toronto. This is not a dream. A chilly wind is blowing. I arrive to line up at five o'clock in the morning, but after a long freezing wait, I get nowhere. The next day I arrive earlier: the same freezing wind, the same result — nothing. The third day I wait all night and I manage to get in, passing through a long tunnel of guards and public servants.

An official asks: "What are you coming to do here?" in a voice that implies I am going to take his money or something even more nefarious. His eyes thunder. I don't know how to answer. Who will translate for me what I feel? In my broken English I reply: "Listen, sir, with all my respect,

I didn't come here because I wanted to. I didn't come to take but to give."
There is so much more that remains unsaid — the treasure I have to
share, the commitment I see myself making and which I indeed already
have. But I reflect nothing but disdain; he reflects nothing but shame.

Amerricua*, my American Continent. For what purpose did I come
so far from my boys and girls, who have disappeared into the mountains
and the streets? So far away from their crazy laughs and their colours
like yours, far away from the contagious rhythms, flavours, women's
breasts with their luscious fruits and perfumes, and our revolutions?
Here I'm going forward, feeling naked again, over a misty platform. My
mouth is shut.

– – – – –

* Amerricua is the original Mayan name from the Atlantic Coasts of
Nicaragua, with which the native Aboriginal peoples were known among
themselves. It is the real, original name from which Alberigo Vespucci
—later self-named Américo Vespucio—took another name and named
the whole continent as: America. Amerricua means "Country (or Land) of
the Winds." America is not the United States of America for the peoples
in "the Americas."

– – – – –

THE SACRIFICED TONGUE

Like the sanctified heart guided by inconceivable love, our tongue sacri-
fices itself by the sacrifice of the word; poetry, chant, and flower. Another
story into my story for you:

Even though the Aztecs were magisterial poets, they confused
this metaphor with reality: when Quetzalcoatl, our divine patriarch,
taught them to "offer the essence and flow of life" to the Giver of Life,
Tonatiuh, the Sun, he never meant us to give up our own blood and that
of our loved ones. This symbol, translated in a strict sense, produced
an abominable dogma. The Aztecs bled their ears, penises, and tongues
with cactus thorns, deceived by a useless notion of "sacrifice." It was an
evil translation (like many others).

My story follows: after recovering and curing my soul by praying, practising yoga, writing, and meditating at the Romero House chapel, after enjoying the miraculous love of my dear friends in that place, I had to move on. Many other souls are now desperately seeking refuge and their lives are at the same risk as mine was.

This is also what I want to translate to my kids like you. Outside, the chilly wind again. I am shipwrecked in the dark winter's ocean. Hailey flies away. Lori goes back to his country. My tongue is numb and hurt by the use of other vowels and meanings. It can't free my soul, not even in the public ESL classrooms for refugees, desperate and lonely students like me; not even at Rideau Hall with its luxurious rooms and hallways. My tongue, like my soul, is still bleeding, shaking sometimes by the echoes of the "dirty war" in the southern rooms of our home: South and Central America. How could I possibly translate for so many children like you, the untranslatable landscapes of my history and my soul?

THE PLUNDERING

Is this just another dream? I'm afraid this is the curse, part of my story I want you to know well.

In our living rooms, in our peaceful homes at the very north of the American continent, we are all relatives and friends. Through the window of our perfect order, we see a group of beautiful creatures like gods, debarking. Your aunt offers them refreshing beverages; the ambassador, your grandfather, gives them his trust and your mom and the rest of you invite them to have a buffet to satisfy their appetite and thirst. Your dad, the Prime Minister, has ordered special rooms for them, artistically decorated, to rest from their journeys through the Heavens. You all give them the best and worship them with incense and songs. Even though you don't understand their holy language, you try to translate the divine intentions of their holy hearts. The story goes on: suddenly they take prisoners — the Pope and his people — and kill them all. They mock and laugh at your precious symbols and humiliate the men after torturing and carving them up — like on a television series — only a few steps from the House of Commons. For months and years to come, more than five centuries, they will rape your precious white daughters, mothers, and sisters; they will demolish your churches and libraries, schools and museums, setting fire to entire cities and villages, burning your books, fashion magazines, and newspapers; they will destroy the art and the sacred meaning of your flowery language, and it goes on and on. They enslave the young, stunning them with unknown hallucinogenic drugs and kill the old men and women, keepers of the traditional knowledge from the Maritimes to British Columbia. From the south to the Northern Territories. Is that okay to you? Is it cool?

Much later, it is now morning and the European Union, the United Nations Corporation, the Northern Empire, and the Holy See declare, unanimously, that they are not disposed to compensate for the damage done by their allies five hundred years ago. Their corporations, always moved by inconceivable generosity, piety, and sweet words, are already negotiating the contracts to rebuild an exclusive tourist paradise, only for "men of good will" and their beloved families. The official language must be sophisticated violence and domestication of the poor. White will be the colour.

A WAVE OF JUNK

The image: over Peru, over Bolivia, over Ecuador, over Panama, and over Colombia; over Central America, Mexico, and the Caribbean crashes a wave of silly songs; war toys; bloody movies; alcohol and cigarettes; new poisoning cults; labels; and televised lies — threatening to obliterate the sacred hearts and minds of children like you. My story shows that there are still wounds from more than five hundred years ago, open and bleeding, infected, poisoned by injustice and lies.

Who would like to translate my stories for you? My twisted mouth is inaccessible to mainstream TV programs. Part of the story is one of bread and circuses for the poor — junk food and commercial television — but the other part is a world of art, culture, and science, high-quality education, philosophy, healthy food, and a life with dignity. Is this only to be made available to some families, and if so, which ones?

Am I still dreaming? I survived on $195 a month for "basic needs" (according to my welfare cheque) and I didn't complain. I know I'm in the struggle. I've been used to buying the cheapest fruit at the cheapest supermarkets (those discount packages that are almost rotten). "Like the ones you have?" I would love to ask you, my dear little neighbour. And I get pasta and cans from the Food Bank; white rice and instant soups. "Like the Prime Minister, the Pope, the politicians from the far, far right or the close, close left?" I would love to ask you and your friends your age sometime.

And I find: even this is a luxurious menu for most of the indigenous families in my country. But where are the nutritious food and the live classical music to resurrect my soul after the storms? Where are the modern dance and the beautiful coloured books for kids like you? Are there not enough for my children in the South? Here I can't enjoy the precious heritage of humankind; a cheap seat at the opera is $75 or $145 (my basic needs!).

Cheese? Almonds? Asiatic philosophy studies or universal culture? These are basic needs to cure my wounds from long, long centuries ago.

But I have another dream in my story (is it a dream or was it real?): I enjoyed a couple of days at a good hotel in Ottawa. Eating incomparable food, listening to incomparable music, sleeping on an incomparable bed, suffering an incomparable loneliness for those, the rest of my beloved at home in the South who will never ever have a piece of this Heaven I had. Instead they deal with a wave of junk (fake news, fake stories for children, fake food) that grows larger with each passing day and that nobody seems to want to mention.

"For us, nothing. Everything for all," the Zapatistas said from the Lacandona jungle. Now it seems like those who are hungry and will not shut up their mouths for justice are "terrorists" according to those who bomb everywhere ... in the name of the white God. Who will catch the storm sometime in the future if we don't dare to say the truth?

THE IMPOSSIBLE HEART

I reveal the passages of my heart to a friend I love, but she runs away, ashamed for the radiance of her heart, terrorized for the vibrant colours of mine and the perfumed cavities of her magic sex. She's an invisible heart. She's a dream. One of the stories I want to be translated for you is this:

On an ice raft, I persist in keeping balance surrounded by the deep ocean and the songs of the sirens.

During my time at Trent University, I returned to live as an urban monk (as I did in Mexico), living in my personal paradise. Here I finish writing the last version of "The colour of the street," that long poetic story of the tragic experiences that street kids have in the Americas.

Why do these children like you live in horror, every day? Who are the Masters who create and preserve that daily horror, in their lives, from positions in the government, organized religion, and untouchable corporations? Do we as well — in some way — support that crime?

I sit for hours at times, naked as I usually do, contemplating the flow of the Otonabee River or the empty wall, all to have the experience of my own mind. At other times I jump for hours, moving my legs and arms in a combat that seems more like a dance of life.

The second part is another story into so many stories — as you can see — where I found myself, on this holy Canadian soil, surrounded by fleeing souls and eyes that don't want to encounter others' eyes. I found intricate sexualities, fearful hearts. They do not stop at my enlightened heart. Am I invisible again? Here there is not a naked sweet hug. My bed is a desert land with cactuses of despair on it.

My daughters are expelled from home. They are forced to go from one side to another. No place to sleep more than a night. Sometimes they eat, sometimes they don't. I feel my soul close to the abyss. I still have my numb tongue and a subtle breath of infinite sadness. Where could I place the colours of my soul? Who and how will translate for you, the silence between my stanzas, hidden in this indomitable language?

A DIVIDED KINGDOM

Dreams and no dreams. Of course Cancún is not Mexico. It's a bubble of impossible dreams for the majority of my people. It is a stylish, ostentatious, and vulgar North American colony. But it is the same in Brazil, Colombia, Santo Domingo, and even Cuba. Behind the dream, under the ground, early in the morning: mothers and children trying to survive from the leftovers of the white people of God. This is part of my story: to tell you that nobody questions the divided order. And my story continues at

George Brown College where I share with students the same questions I would like to share with you and your mother:

"What's the most important thing for you in life? What's the most important thing for the politicians, religious leaders, business executives, and television producers who set the work for you? Is their most important value, you? Or is it money?" I know you know. But maybe Mom is afraid of knowing a truth that you already know. Is there any wrong in knowing something everybody knows?

I try not to hate anyone. Not even those who planned the second Holocaust in Latin America by chasing, torturing, disappearing, and killing thousands of families for one sin: not thinking as they think. Not seeing people, nature, education, health, culture, religion, philosophy, entertainment, and so on, as money. It is hard really not to hate anyone. I try to deal amid a fight between two sides attacking each other.

My daughters resist. Ivana, the younger one, cannot sleep in peace. Nightmares throw her to the abyss. She misses me; I miss her. She cries and so do I, even as an adult, but that doesn't change even when we are so far apart. Have you passed through that? Well, you don't have to!

Who will translate the next of my stories for the many other children: will it be those who possess, rule, and lead with that unthinkable abundance of money? Those who have new cars, radiant wives, expensive lovers, healthy sons, high-class culture, and privileged access to pompous universities? Those who take vacations every year, served by us or our families: refugees, miserable or persecuted for our ideas ... do you think they will publish our visions, living in this mansion of global exploitation? What is the language, the sounds, visions, and values we must learn to be translated?

Our heart is still invisible in this divided kingdom.

THE HIDDEN HOLOCAUST

In the roads lie the broken spears ...
Without roofs are the houses,
And red are their walls with blood
Maggots swarm in the streets and squares,
And the ramparts are spattered with brains
— from *Elegy for Tenochtitlan,* anonymous, 1528

You couldn't dream that those beautiful creatures like gods —
white skin and unknown hearts — came into our cities from Europe.
Those stories, not dreams but real stories, are part of my own story for
you, and are nearly identical whether written in the Aztec and Mayan
codexes or preserved by the Inca elders, by the Cherokees, Muiscas,
Diaguitas, Navajos, the Iroquois, or the inhabitants of Cuba and Haiti.
They all suffered in similar ways from those representatives of the white
kings and the unique white God. And now, it seems like they just forgot!
They don't want to talk about it. They have so many new problems.

It has been planned, intentionally, consistently, from then to now;
extermination, murder, disappearance. Children like you, and their families like yours, are now paying for what was done five hundred years ago;
half a century ago; and in the 1970s.

Will there be nobody to restore the damage? No international justice to address these wrongs? An entire house was stolen: what about if it
were the prime minister's, the General Secretary of the United Nations',
the Pope's, or the U.S. president's house that was plundered? Would
any of them let the Conquerors again do what they did to the original
inhabitants of this land?

Maybe you don't have to know the full names of the Big Bad Wolf
and his comrades from the International Monetary Fund and the World
Bank. Maybe you don't have to know the names and addresses of the
Dragons of Drugs; but, should you know that he's setting a trap for you
and your friends with his TV channels of mental junk? My story is starting to get scary now ... let me introduce you to Mr. Augusto Pinochet
in Chile; Mr. Henry Kissinger and Mr. Ronald Reagan and Mr. Richard
Nixon in the U.S.; no longer heroes but sophisticated murderers, apparently untouchable by any system of justice in the world.

Maybe Mom prefers you to fill your sophisticated, beautiful head
with Britney Spears hair colour or the silly or heavy songs of a bunch
of plastic boys and artificial girls. As I said before to my street kids in
Mexico: "I don't want you to suffer, but this is the truth." And what is
neither a story nor a dream is that the new Conquerors do not want us
to translate and show you our own history. They are taking prisoners
again, our children and young, and they are raping and killing — in so
many sophisticated ways — our girls and boys. Stealing again and again
your sons' and daughters' water, woods, oceans, jungles, lives, and seeds
and thoughts in the name of God the Almighty Father, his corporations,

and the modern-day kings of Europe — in a hypocritical bath of purity and democracy.

Will the merciful God allow the miracle to translate what the refugee poet, the journalist from another land, the novelist from nowhere, the African or Asian philosopher, the dramatist with skin of ebony, sky, and jungle colours has to say? Or is God only white and dressed with money?

CHARITY AND SLAVERY

More dreams of piety, its images. The Good Will World organizes enormous efforts to raise money for "the unfortunate poor of the earth." The minds and hearts of those who enjoy and organize such endeavours haven't noticed that perhaps they are just prisoners of their greed, fear, and spiritual ignorance. They don't really want to share what they really know is best: They pray but they do not dare to change the wheel of history by laying the foundation of true justice on the same shores that their ancestors sowed with crime and discord. Another image: On a piece of ice, after the previous combat, I take a breath without letting down my saber, trying to recognize the invisible signs of my uncertain future.

At George Brown College my heart is safe. In the classrooms I share with single mothers, excellent young women, wise seniors, impetuous young men from all over the world, they receive my intense words openly and respectfully. Some of them still show their war wounds in their souls. They are victims of the same new Empire of money and greed.

That's why I love to write and to talk, in my stories, about a Simple Revolution. This is a political and spiritual revolution; but is about neither political parties nor religions. It is just about reassuring those universal values that bond us together. It is a true Mexican fiesta! A celebration and returning to life. Not about smashing people for "good reasons," but about freeing ourselves from the addiction to consuming all those products that come from human exploitation.

Only that: a Simple Revolution. In my story you will notice that we don't need charity anymore. No slavery to drugs, strict ideas, junk food, junk news, junk thoughts, again. No more religious or political junk but justice and universal values. All we want our children to enjoy we should get for every child in our own home: the American Continent.

Is it disturbing to translate such thoughts like these for you? Are you and your friends afraid, after seeing ten thousand hours of horror and crime on the big and little screens, hundreds of killings in Nintendo and more killings and bombings of unarmed innocents and sacred places all around the globe? Are you afraid of knowing the real causes of those killings?

GOD'S OBLIVION

An image: God's forgetfulness is our oblivion. We forgot to translate all the sacred languages; those that were the languages of poetry, transcendence, precise meaning, and above all, truth.

We forgot the reflection of God in our daily lives and its habits: God doesn't buy or sell. God does not exploit nor hoard up. God never bombs nor lies nor steals for any "reason." God doesn't pay publicists and TV channels or newspapers to exalt Its image.

We've forgotten to translate into our lives the black flavour of the real history of humankind; the Aboriginal flavour, the eastern flavour and many other flavours. We've forgotten to translate prolifically the mother languages and their sacred impulse. In my stories to you, it is possible to find that we forgot to ask the refugee, on the afternoon after he arrives, if he has eaten, if she is tired, if he needs a kiss, if she needs a hug or some passionate night, long until the dawn, with blessed love and sex. Why not? This is part of adult life. We only ask: "Hi, how are you?" in a mechanical act and never ask: "How is your soul today?"

We push him/her to chew and swallow another language in order to survive, knowing that soon he/she'll be invisible again, working as a servant in our fields, washrooms, restaurants, and other low-paid service jobs. Rarely working as a doctor, teacher, philosopher, writer, director, actor, president, journalist or so forth. We teach him/her the supreme value of being an article of merchandise in a stolen continent. We forget his/her daughters and sons and nieces; her/his written or oral stories and ancestors. We forget, intentionally, to translate her/his thoughts, to let him/her recover his/her original colours and to share them with children like you. We forget about God because we've already eaten enough, because our world is safe and the TV is on.

But, in my story, the world will continue. A bunch of arrogant and madly violent fools will not destroy this marvellous planet at all. They have not that spiritual power. But a miracle will not happen, and will not save, free, or liberate you from the ignorance of our highest human values and pain.

Now I'm rehearsing a new translation of truth for children like you. The truth that you are the sacred heritage of humankind. Your truth, the amazing truths everybody has, and the very truth that ... you are the truth! In the middle of an immense ocean of darkness, you are still the truth!

RECONCILIATION

No dreams at all. To affirm, to deny, to reconcile: a universal law.

This is Acadia University, "an oasis of peace," said Rev. Prentice. My daughters came to visit me in Toronto before I arrived here. We are learning to rebuild the new temple of our love. They went back to their combat, into their lives. They are learning how to live in paradise ... even in hell!

Sometimes I can't remember all of the protest songs I've learned. Where are my revolutions? I'm forgetting the Mayan, Aztec, Olmec sacred names, thinking: "Where will I sleep tomorrow?" "Where can my daughters grow and shine like a sun?"

I've been looking for another language for my stories to you. I want to translate a new path. No hopes, no dreams for me. Hopes and dreams, in my stories, are just a weak and mediocre bunch of useless good intentions. Cemeteries, prisons, streets, madhouses, government and religious buildings are full of hopes and dreams. Nothing has changed with those. Nothing will.

I prefer to wake up. My very open eyes. My bed is still empty like a desert, but who cares? I don't, and as I see another holy Canadian sunset, I know: the sun in my heart is here to share. This part of my story for you and your friends, made up from many stories, ends when suddenly I stop dreaming because, even sleeping, I am awake!

Stella Lee and Alan Cumyn

Searching in Translation

The world changes in a day, but how do you explain this to people, and how do you translate the experience across cultures when you can hardly understand it yourself?

I will always remember that Sunday afternoon four years ago. On a whim, my husband, Jiang Weiping, decided to drive me and our daughter, Jiang Yue, to the beach. We drove along the coastal highway of Dalian, our home in China. He suggested a special outing to take photos for our daughter's upcoming birthday. The weather in early December was a bit chilly, but it was still beautiful and sunny. We walked along the beach talking about writing and taking photos. We didn't go to the beach very often because Weiping was so busy with his work as a journalist. That afternoon we chatted so much it was almost dark by the time we drove back downtown. While waiting for our pictures to be developed, we went to a small restaurant for dinner. The photograph I have gazed at most often since that trip is of Weiping himself. He is smiling in his easy way for the camera, a bit of wind in his hair, the large sea behind.

The next morning was terribly cold and it began to snow. Instead of taking the bus, Weiping drove us, first Yue to her school and then me to my office, where I was assistant to the general manager at a travel agency. I had worked as an interpreter before that and had travelled to many countries with my job. The task of translating between cultures was not new to me. But what about translating between realities — when the world I thought I knew suddenly became something else?

I was ill-prepared for that, as many of us would be.

I remember I was in a negative mood because of some problems at work. Weiping, wanting to cheer me up, said that if he didn't have too much to do that day he could probably pick me up at five o'clock and we could go out to dinner and see a film. Weiping used to be the China bureau chief for the Hong Kong-based *Wen Hui Bao*, but since leaving the paper, he continued to maintain an office in downtown Dalian, writing freelance for other publications. His days were busy, and often he wasn't certain what he would be writing about until the phone rang and a story developed. But his schedule seemed light that Monday morning. It was still early when he dropped me off, so he said he would return home for a while before going to his office.

As it turned out, I wasn't very busy that afternoon, so I called him on his cellphone. There was no answer. I called his office and tried his beeper — no response. Normally, if Weiping couldn't talk to me right away he would return my call within a few minutes. But I heard nothing from him.

I waited at my office past five o'clock, but he didn't arrive. As a journalist he often got called away on sudden assignments. Probably something urgent had come up, I thought. I took a taxi back home, cooked beef soup for our dinner, and waited for him. By seven o'clock there was still no call, and I began to feel terribly uneasy. This was not normal at all. I tried all of his phone numbers. Ten o'clock came and went. Unable to eat, I returned to the phone. Terrible thoughts ran through my head as I imagined he had had an accident or perhaps had been kidnapped. Recently several taxi drivers in our city had been killed and their cars taken away. It could happen to any of us.

After midnight, I began to call some of his close friends. They all said they hadn't seen him that day. At two in the morning, barely holding back tears, I called his elder brother, who remained calm and reasoned that Weiping probably had had to go somewhere suddenly and was unable to get in touch with me. Now it was late and I should just get some sleep, he told me. Weiping would contact me when he could.

I could not sleep, and instead I paced back and forth in our room. This had never happened to us before. Weiping had always found a way to let me know where he was, even when he was called away to cover some terrible accident. The next morning, I called my sister and brother-in-law, and together we phoned the local officials who deal with roads and highways. We wanted to see if there had been a bad accident or some other serious event that Weiping had either been involved in or might be covering.

No one seemed to know of such a thing.

The hours passed in terrible silence. I tried to think of what to do. As a correspondent, Weiping had covered three provinces in northern China: Liaoning, Heilongjiang, and Jilin. I looked in his telephone books at home and began calling his contacts long distance at a horrible expense. No one knew where he was. Slowly, the day tightened like the twisting of a rope.

Then, strangely, at about two o'clock in the afternoon I remembered a conversation we had had a year before. Beginning in 1998, Weiping had written a series of articles exposing high-level government corruption, and he said this work would probably bring him trouble some day. Usually he showed me his writing, but I didn't see those articles. And he said little because he didn't want to upset or worry me. But he did tell me not to talk about private things on the phone. According to his sources, he was on the list of journalists to be closely watched by the local security bureau.

So a small part of me was not surprised when the phone rang and a man from the state security bureau informed me that they would come around to my home very shortly. My younger sister was staying with me by then. About ten officers arrived and began searching my apartment. I was angry and demanded to know why they were searching our home. They said Weiping was under detention for harming state security, and they presented a paper for me to sign. I refused. I knew Weiping would never truly do anything against his country. Certainly his work was an embarrassment to the government, but Weiping was serving the larger interests of his nation, not threatening it.

For eight hours, until midnight, the state security officials searched our apartment and my husband's office. They took Weiping's diaries and notebooks as well as our family albums and books. It was a violation of our privacy, our lives, and I was helpless to intervene.

Much later, when some of my husband's prison letters reached me through underground channels, I learned what had happened that day. In fact, my husband had not been so much arrested as kidnapped by the police. After he had dropped me off at my office, he returned to our apartment. Four people grabbed him in the parking lot, wrapped his overcoat over his head, and shoved him in a car. He was held incommunicado for forty-eight days. It was impossible to see him or to get him a lawyer. I was told that he was in Dalian prison so I went there regularly, but I never saw his name on the prisoner rolls, and of course I did not see him.

An arrest of this kind in China used to be called a counter-revolutionary crime; now it is known as harming state security. Friends, colleagues, and family members are also endangered. My two sisters' houses were searched because they kept close contact with me. Many friends, without saying anything explicit, began to keep their distance for their own safety. Even close relatives started to treat us differently. Privately, many people expressed disbelief that my husband had done anything wrong, yet the authorities hold a great deal of power in these matters. We were all very frightened. North Americans can hardly imagine this level of daily fear, how a family member can disappear this way, and how everyone's life is stained.

The one piece of good news that came after my husband's arrest was a letter from the Canadian consulate inviting me to Hong Kong for an interview. The meeting was regarding an immigration application I had made years before and, quite frankly, had forgotten about, as the process had taken so long. I travelled secretly to Hong Kong, bringing with me clippings about Weiping's arrest. The Canadian immigration officer was very sympathetic and assured me that a visa would be forthcoming. I returned home and waited for word of my husband and my future.

I could not attend Weiping's trial, which was held in secret in September 2001. He was found guilty of inciting to overthrow the government and revealing state secrets. It did not seem to matter that a month later the Shenyang mayor, who had been stripped of his post and Communist Party membership, was found guilty of corruption and sentenced to death.

Weiping's sentence was for eight years. Soon after the verdict was announced I lost my job at the travel agency. I understood quite well that I was let go because I was now the wife of a convicted political prisoner. Then, in March 2002, I was held in detention in much the same way as Weiping had been. The Committee to Protect Journalists (CPJ) in New York had given Weiping the 2001 International Press Freedom Award, which publicized his case around the world. I was accused of revealing the secrets of my husband's case to foreign journalists. Taken to a secret house, I was watched and questioned for twenty-seven days. Six women and three men watched me on shift to prevent my escape.

Our daughter, who was only twelve years old, was terrified during this time, so she stayed with my sister. Even after I was released and returned home, she dared not speak aloud inside our apartment in case anyone was listening. She always wanted to go outside to talk, and she was afraid to hear her father's name mentioned at home. Also, she was so afraid that I could be taken away again that she kept calling me to make sure I was safe. She used to be such an outgoing, happy girl, but her parents' arrest had shaken her deeply, and my heart was aching.

We had to leave. I no longer felt safe in my own country, and I didn't want my daughter to live in such fear. Our peaceful life had totally changed. It also occurred to me that even when Weiping was released, he would not actually get his freedom, much like other political prisoners. He would remain under close surveillance — and who would dare hire him?

It is one thing to come to a decision to leave China and quite another to accomplish it. After my release I was required to report to the Public Security Bureau for permission to travel anywhere outside Dalian, even to visit my ill father. Leaving the country was out of the question. Besides that, my visa still had not arrived. After a year, the travel restriction was lifted, although I still felt like I was being monitored. Finally, in the fall of 2003, the visa came through. To arouse as little suspicion as possible, I booked two tickets on a tour to South Korea, rather than booking a direct flight to Canada. My daughter and I stayed in a Seoul hotel for a couple of days, and then we approached a Canadian official at the airport. With our visa, and the kindness of Canadian officials, we were finally on our way to Canada.

How well I remember the trip to Toronto to begin a new life. The airport at midnight was spacious and silent. The only voice reverberating in the large area came from the loudspeaker. My brain felt packed with cotton batting and I could barely make out the words. On the way to my friend's house — where we would stay while I found my feet — everything in my field of vision was covered by thick white snow. As we passed buildings and houses, the dim light was soft and mysterious, both familiar and strange. I had visited Toronto in the late 1980s as an interpreter for the Dalian Acrobatic Troupe. Everything in Toronto had looked so new and strange to me. On the streets, I had observed young long-haired boys wearing blue jeans, girls in short skirts with high-heeled shoes, elderly ladies in colourful clothes and heavy make-up. At McDonald's, people sat leisurely eating big hamburgers with that strange dark-coloured drink — Coca-Cola. In China, I had been criticized at school as being "bourgeois" just for wearing a pink dress while everyone else was in blue or grey. Yet in the intervening years, so many of these trappings of capitalism had become popular in China. Now I was in exile, fleeing from a country that looked Western but inside it remained as allergic to criticism as in its overtly communist days.

It seemed that the snow would never stop falling once I decided to begin a new life in Toronto. I rented a small second-floor room in a house for me and my daughter. The only furniture was a used mat on the ground. From the window I could see Canadian children my daughter's age playing in the snow.

I knew the beginning would be very hard for us. It turned out to be even more difficult than I had expected. Living expenses are so high in Canada. The money I brought with me drained away. To ease the financial strain, I began looking for a job. I sent out hundreds of resumes, all of which seemed to sink into the sea. During those long winter days I went from one workshop to another — learning computer skills, language training, job interview strategies — but without results. I could not contact my husband, and it seemed hopeless that he would be freed anytime soon. I felt very discouraged. At the same time, a Chinese friend and her husband who had settled in Toronto both lost their jobs. They stayed at home for almost a year receiving Employment Insurance from the government. "There are a lot of people like us. Probably it's better for you to apply for it, too," my friend suggested. But that's not the way I wanted to start my new life.

Even now, one year later, the simplest aspects of life can seem difficult. Every time I go to a grocery store I get a headache just trying to read and understand the instructions on the back of each item. Although I am trained as an interpreter, using a second language in a new country is still challenging. I have found that many immigrants from China never learn to speak English. They go to Chinese groceries, eat at Chinese restaurants, read Chinese newspapers, and associate with the people from their home country. But how can we become a part of this society if we stay separate all the time? After moving to Canada, I threw myself into learning everything new, took as many classes as I could afford, read the English newspapers, and made Canadian friends. I have tried very hard to "translate" myself completely into this new country. As well, I have tried to find pleasure from living as an immigrant in Canada. I work at a Chinese grocery store now, preparing sushi. I never prepared sushi before, but I have learned, and like many immigrants before me, I will do whatever it takes to gain a foothold here for my own sake and my family's.

But how do I translate my strange history as the wife of a political prisoner for others to understand? I work with other Chinese immigrants, and I stay quiet about my husband's problems. It is a delicate matter. For one thing, new immigrants are struggling so hard just to live, they don't want to know about others' troubles. Many of them were skilled professionals back in China, but in Canada the only work open to them is menial. So, they are poor and exhausted and often not very happy about coming to Canada. Even though they live in Canada, Chinese immigrants can be suspicious and feel that they are not safe from Chinese authorities. Because of this, I do not want to burden my colleagues with the knowledge that my husband is in prison. I'm not sure how they would react, so I keep quiet about my past. Many of us still have relatives in China and, for their sake, we are afraid to raise our voices in criticism, even from abroad.

My Canadian friends tend to be very sympathetic towards my story. But it is hard for a native-born Canadian to really understand the way things work in China, the level of repression that can swallow individuals and make them afraid to speak out. It's difficult to understand the impossibility of defending oneself in China once the authorities have turned against you. Perhaps the best way I have to translate this experience clearly to others is through organizations such as the Committee to Protect Journalists and PEN Canada. So many lovely people from these and other groups have been so helpful; it has given me the confidence to speak out and continue with my struggle. Not just my husband, but many people have been unjustly imprisoned and need our help. The work is exhausting, but it must be done.

Yet a part of me, of course, still yearns to be back on the beach in Dalian on that Sunday afternoon that now seems so distant. Weiping, Yue, and I are walking together, the weather is fine, and the air full of the scent of the ocean. We are going to take pictures for Yue's birthday, and the world seems calm, safe, and understandable, as anyone can see, with or without translation. We will reach that day again; not in Dalian, I'm afraid, but somewhere else, I know, as surely as I know anything any more.

Senthilnathan Ratnasabapathy

Translating the Global Language

What is translation? The online Webster's Dictionary states that to translate is "to turn into one's own or another language" or "to express in different terms and especially different words" or "to paraphrase." The emphasis is on interpreting one language into another.

In my view, this definition is too traditional and conservative. How about translating a word or phrase in the same language, from one culture to another? For example, in parts of Sri Lanka, where I hail from, the expression "you bugger" is commonly used, but elsewhere it could raise eyebrows. One will have to translate from English to English to impart the appropriate meaning. In Britain it might be "lucky sod," in Canada perhaps "you lucky bastard" — though even then we have to take into account the need to translate terms between different social groups in the same country or else end up giving offence.

As distances shrink in these times of high-speed communication and mass transcontinental movement of goods and people, we also witness cultures interacting with one another in an unprecedented way. Even Hollywood is forced to accept characters from distant cultures. Take the Hollywood production *Guru*. It was not the best production to come out of the world's largest film industry, and one could certainly argue about whether it did any good for the Indian spiritual tradition, but it was an effort to take the issue of migrants and their cultural background seriously, even including a song and dance sequence, usually a Bollywood trait. The film *Bend It Like Beckham* went a step further

— here was a film that clearly went beyond the "India equals curry" notion and portrayed the changing pattern of immigration, where most of the immigrants to First World nations are not from other First World nations but from the Third World — and looked at how immigrants, their cultures, and their traditions can be taken seriously by mainstream.

Therefore, it's logical that the term "translation" should also mean interpreting the same words from one culture to another. The need for this is painfully clear when it comes to visa applications. One English dictate that has caused great aggravation for thousands of citizens from the so-called Third World is to "prove that you will return home." This has to be paired with another term frequently found on visa applications: "genuine tourist."

Simply put, or translated, the first dictate means that if you wish to visit a country on a temporary basis — for study, tourism, or whatever reason — you have to prove that you intend not to abuse the terms under which the visa is granted. By the specified deadline, you must leave that country and return to your home country before the visa expires. The burden of proving this point falls to the applicant.

Sounds simple and logical, doesn't it?

It isn't.

Most of the developing nations have simplified visa requirements for Western citizens. Some do not require any visa, just a valid passport, for Western citizens on short-term business or visitor trips. Some stamp you a three-month visa at the port of entry. Few countries, such as India, hang onto the principle of reciprocity in that they will waive the visa policy for a certain country's citizens if that country returns the favour.

Citizens of a few developing nations such as Malaysia do not need visas to visit a number of rich countries. For the rest of the Third World citizens — that is, for the vast majority of the world's humanity — visiting a rich country remains a dream, even if they have more wealth than many in the West could dream of.

Why? Because there appears to be a globally accepted way of translating visa terms from one culture's English to another's. One would hope that this uniformity might help immigration officers to be flexible, but many would argue this has helped some immigration officers to be irrational and often racist.

For example, take the case of a Sri Lankan who wanted to attend his niece's wedding in Canada. He owned a house, a car, and other property in

Sri Lanka and held a plum job in the financial sector, one of those jobs where a "peon" opens the door of the car, takes your bag, brings you tea or coffee, and even does your grocery shopping for you. To further support his case, he attached a letter of invitation sent by the niece's eldest sister, successfully settled down in Canada. Yet the high commission in Colombo rejected his application. The compassionate officer decided that this upper-middle-class Sri Lankan would add an extra burden to the niece, who not only had to take care of him for a month during his stay in Canada but also her bride-to-be sister as well as her brother-in-law!

Or take the case of a colleague of mine in Sri Lanka who wanted to send his only son for higher education in the UK. That Sri Lanka has known more war than peace in the past two decades is a well-known story, but many do not know that those in the northern and eastern part of the island have faced the worst violence.

But in the late 1980s, southern Sri Lanka, too, flared up in violence as a rebel group launched a campaign against the government. As a journalist, one of my duties was to keep a tally of bodies, often headless, that were strewn on roadsides, in the woods, or floating down rivers and in coastal waters. Most of the victims were youths who had nothing to do with rebellion. Tragically, those from the ranks of the government who organized the counter-offensive against the campaign decided that the best way to solve the issue was to kill as many youths as possible.

My colleague wanted to send his son abroad to keep him alive. Having passed the relevant British qualifying exams, the young man was accepted by a British university. But his visa application was rejected because there was no proof he would return to Sri Lanka once he'd completed his studies. As the only child in the family, he did not have to work to live in luxury; his family owned enough property in the country to last for generations. Yet, he could not convince the visa officer that he was a "genuine" student.

I left Sri Lanka as a refugee, crossing borders — legally when they did not demand visas from Sri Lankan citizens and illegally when they did — and thus was spared any such experiences. But eventually I was granted enough opportunities to test my skills in "translation." When I was finally granted asylum with permanent residence in Austria, I applied for and received the so-called Travel Document, a grey passport with black stripes — to some, the sign of poverty, despair, and oppression.

I was in an strange situation: I was still legally a citizen of a Third World nation, but I enjoyed certain First World rights. Neither fish nor fowl. I was an "Auslander" who had no political rights and whose experience working for Sri Lankan and foreign media could get me only a job selling newspapers because no Austrian would touch it. Yet labour laws allowed me to take up any job anywhere within Austria, and I was considered by law an equal in many social and economic spheres in this rich country. The refugee status and the Travel Document gave me also one privilege that many foreigners lacked — I could travel to anywhere in the world. Except Sri Lanka.

I had to test my new-found status, however confusing it was. So I travelled to Bratislava, the capital of Slovakia. Bratislava is just an hour's train journey from Vienna, capital of Austria. As a holder of an Austrian TD, I did not need a visa.

But the TD must have confused the Slovak border officials; they held hurried meetings and went through books before letting me in without testing these terms on me.

Then I decided on my next trip, to Bulgaria. This was more complicated, partly because I needed a visa and partly because I wanted to go as a writer. It's one of my weaknesses; whenever I visit a place, I need to write at least one story with that dateline. To help out in such cases, various embassies and consulates post diplomats as media officers; the Bulgarian media officer was very helpful.

At the airport in Sophia, however, things were different. I was supposed to enter the country with confirmed accommodation, but I lacked that. The immigration officers were very determined to make me prove that I was not in Bulgaria for the sole purpose of becoming an illegal immigrant. Fortunately, with all the money I had, I managed to make them believe that I was indeed a "genuine tourist." This was my first experience with the visa procedure: I successfully translated the terms!

Now I was onto my next adventure, which I thought would be the most risky. I was studying at the Open University in the UK and had to attend a week of intense study in the summer. I realized it was time to confront Sri Lanka's former colonizer, to visit the country that gave us the English language, tea, the railways, the multi-party democratic system, the core of our pre-university educational system with Ordinary Levels and Advanced Levels (which, incidentally, has since changed in the "mother" country), and many other cultural heirlooms, including a deadly ethnic war. And for a bookworm, Britain is a heaven.

Both in Sri Lanka and in Austria I had bought UK-published books, and they always had two prices: one printed, usually in the back cover, with the pound sign and the other either labelled or simply written. There was always a huge difference between the first and the second, and I had assumed that this entailed not just the conversion from one currency to the other, taxes, transportation, and labour charges but maybe even the upkeep costs for the staff of the bookstores. But now I was planning to go to a country where I could buy books for the original price. Even that thought sent my brain into high gear, thinking of the books I needed.

Nurturing the desire to visit the UK is one thing, but getting the visa is another. Third World nations are full of stories of how tough it could be to convince a British visa officer that you are a "genuine" traveller or immigrant. In the 1970s, the country ran "virginity" tests: literal examinations to verify the virginity of newlywed South Asian women brides who came to the UK to join their husbands. The presumption was that South Asian women never have sexual intercourse prior to the marriage. Immigration officials now sometimes seem to apply their own sort of virginity tests to applicants. A couple I know had applied to visit London. Both of them had good jobs, owned a house in Sri Lanka, and their bank balances were impressive. Even while many of their professional compatriots migrated abroad because of the civil war, they refused to leave Sri Lanka. He in particular was not fond of going abroad, and they both had spurned many a chance to go to the West as refugees. But now they wanted to go to London for the sole reason to attend the wedding of their eldest son, a naturalized British citizen. Not only their parental feelings but also Hindu traditions required their presence. But when they applied for the visa, the visa officer in Colombo somehow could not imagine that they were "genuine."

Such stories are common in Sri Lanka, and they ran through my mind as I contemplated applying for a visa. And having your visa application turned down is no small matter. Your records are archived, and the next time you apply for a visa, the previous application will come down to haunt you. And God knows with how many countries Britain shares this information.

But I was also a different kind of species, somewhere between the Third and First Worlds. For starters, I was to travel not on a Third World passport, but on a First World Travel Document and that was advantage number one. I had been living in Austria for five years, which meant I could apply for citizenship, and that was advantage number two because, so the theory would go, if I were eligible for Austrian citizenship, the chances I would stay as an illegal immigrant in Britain were low.

Besides, I was going on legitimate business. I imagined it wouldn't be difficult to correctly translate the term "genuine" visitor for the visa officer.

However, I also had some disadvantages: I did not own any property and I was still theoretically a citizen of a Third World country whose many citizens were applying for asylum in Britain. More than that, my more-than-one-job situation would confound the visa officers.

But I prepared meticulously. I made several photocopies of the visa application form and ran trials. Simple spelling mistakes could make things worse.

I was ready to face the interview. I guessed the questions that the visa officer would ask and prepared answers. The key points were that I should not contradict myself and should be confident. When I appeared at the embassy, the visa officer blinked her eyes, saying, "So many documents!" — I had cheques and bank statements from my newspaper in India, from Singapore, from the Viennese office of the international news service I was writing for, a letter from the director of the news agency in Vienna, letters from the Open University, my rent documents. It was the whole lot.

I got the visa. I could be proud of my English. I had successfully proved the point that I would return once my business in the country was over.

I knew I now belonged to an elite club of Third World citizens — citizens who could travel to the UK, which effectively meant they could travel to any part of the First World. But I wondered who would I be without my Travel Document and my English.

A few years later, I travelled farther: to Brazil for the whole month of February. It was not only to expand my horizons and to work, but also to escape the lugubrious Viennese winter.

I needed a visa, whether I went as a tourist or as a journalist. I preferred the journalistic visa route because, I assumed, it would be given more priority and respect. Who wants to offend a scribe, after all? But the visa officer at the Brazilian embassy subtly recommended that I apply for a tourist visa. I dutifully did my paperwork, including booking a hotel in São Paolo and buying up the necessary traveller's cheques. Besides letters and other proofs from my employers, I also attached a copy of a credit card statement declaring my credit limit. When I finally made my application, I was asked to come back the next day for the result. Twenty fours hours! Would I get it? Did I manage to convince him that I was a "genuine" tourist who would not stay back in Brazil? What happens if I didn't get it? These questions haunted me that night.

I did get the visa. Even though the visa officer and I both came from cultures where English was not the lingua franca, and even though I was not as meticulous in my preparations as I had been with my UK visa application, I managed without difficulty to prove the terms of my application. Or was it because the visa officer was more pragmatic and had decided that I would not give up my privileged permanent residency in Austria to live in Brazil? But I could not think that immigration officers are that rational. I knew only too well the struggle I had with the Bulgarian immigration officials to prove that I was a "genuine" tourist. I had also run into the same type of troubles with Slovenian authorities a little later, as I tried to enter the country to cover a conference on human rights. I had checked with the Slovene embassy in Vienna and was informed that as a TD holder, I did not need a visa for my three-day visit. But despite that fact, and despite the fact that I possessed more than enough money to live in Slovenia for a month, I had trouble convincing the border official that I was just travelling to cover a conference and not to apply for asylum.

So what was it that convinced the Brazilian visa officer in Vienna and the relevant ministry in Brasilia to grant me the visa? A sort of Third World solidarity that ran through them? Or simply that they were bureaucrats who wanted to apply the law fairly — as long as I fulfilled their conditions, they were happy?

Brazil turned out to be one of the most memorable trips I have ever made. As I had my exit visa stamped at the airport in São Paulo a month later, I realized that this was one country that should have made a big fuss about granting me a visa. If I had had a job there, I would have stayed.

My plane from São Paolo landed at the Heathrow airport early in the day, and as I had more than a few hours until my flight to Vienna, I decided to do some sightseeing in London. Unlike many Third World citizens, I did not need a visa to land in the UK while in transit, but to leave the airport, I needed one. This was tricky, because I should have applied before leaving Vienna.

Nevertheless, I decided to try my luck and went to the immigration counter to ask for a few hours of visa. I had gone ahead to the terminal from where the Viennese flight was to leave; the officer reminded me that I should have asked for the visa at the immigration counter at the terminal where my plane had landed. I apologized.

"What do you want to do in the city?"

"I want to buy some English books and software."

Raised eyebrows.

"Why?"

"Because one can get the books at a lower price."

"Where exactly?"

"I want to go to Victoria Station, come out, and there is a big book store selling lots of books at bargain prices."

Was there surprise in the officer's eye? Obviously, he realized I had been to the bookshop before.

"You really should have applied at the other terminal."

"Well, I suddenly decided to go to the city. If it is too much trouble, I don't need it."

I asked for a few hours, but got a visa for three months!

This was my third trip to the UK. My first two were study-related, and each time I received the visa, my sense of belonging to the elite club only increased.

Alas, reality soon caught up with me, and it came from an unexpected source.

An old acquaintance of mine was living in Norway and ran an import-export business. He wanted to expand into Southeast Asian countries. Since I know a lot about this region, he asked me whether I could visit him to talk about business opportunities. He promised to pay for the ticket.

Who would say no? But being a journalist, I also wanted to do a few stories. I was writing for media outlets that dealt with developing world themes, and Norway was considered one of the "progressive" developed nations when it came to aid, human rights, etc. It was Christmas time — the Scandinavian country was about to close down — but still I managed to coax Norway's foreign media department to arrange some interviews.

I applied for the necessary visa. The Norwegian embassy in Vienna did not have a visa section, but the counsellor who accepted the application was very friendly and gave me some story ideas as well. The visa had to be approved in Oslo, but she promised to push for an early decision.

Then came the shock. The visa was rejected. The officials in Oslo did not think that my visit was genuinely touristic. They had their doubts about whether I would return after the visit.

The counsellor at the embassy in Vienna shared my surprise. I called my friend. He said someone from the relevant ministry had called to ask whether he knew me. He had taken up his former Norwegian wife's last name, but said the moment the official realized it was in fact a Third World citizen with a Norwegian name, the tone changed. Apparently, there was a contradiction between what he said and what I said. He said I was coming on a business trip as a consultant, while I said I was going on a journalism trip with the consultation as a side issue. There was a misunderstanding, leading to a breakdown in the communication.

On my return from Brazil, I appealed and lost. I fumed.

At first, I thought I would write a long letter outlining what I felt was a humiliation and wanted to send it to the Norwegian prime minister, justice minister, and all the media. I just needed to get one newspaper to publish my story.

Instead I gave up. I was fighting a new system, the Schengen Agreement, set up by many European nations to deal with asylum and immigration applications. It was based on exclusion — that is, it looks not for reasons to grant the visa (or refugee status) but for reasons to deny it. In my case, yes, there was a contradiction because while both my acquaintance and myself gave both reasons for my travel to Norway, our emphases differed. But was that grave enough to deny the visa? A call to the counsellor in Vienna or to me would have clarified the issue. I had clearly stated that I was going to do both, and had even mentioned the names of officers from the foreign media department. They just had to call them to confirm it. Besides, I was working for an international news agency and with proven accreditation in Austria. Why would I lie to go to Norway? Part of me, the part with rage, urged me to go ahead with the letter, but the other part wanted me to give up. It was a battle between my own sense of injustice and my "let it go" attitude. The latter won.

Sharryn Aiken, former director of the Summer Course on Refugee Studies at the York University, has ample experience with the irrationality of the visa regime. Two years in a row, she saw some of the applicants being turned down. Usually from Africa and Asia, their academic and professional credentials were excellent, and they could also furnish letters from their employers that they had their jobs when they returned. Yet, they would be denied the visa.

Years ago I remember reading an article about the situation Prof. Amartya Sen, the eminent Indian economist, found himself in. After receiving the Nobel Price for Economics, Sen, who made a name for analyzing the relationship between democracy, people's participation, and development, was invited to speak at the Davos Forum in Switzerland. Still holding his Indian passport, he landed in Switzerland after being told by Swiss officials in London that he could get a visa once he landed in the country. The officials at the airport, however, refused him a visa, perhaps thinking that this elderly man was an illegal immigrant wanting to apply for asylum. High-ranking Swiss officials had to intervene before Prof. Sen was let go, according to the report.

If Prof. Sen, a Harvard professor, former Master of Trinity College in Cambridge, and a Nobel Laureate, could not successfully translate the terms of a "genuine tourist" for the Swiss officials to understand, then where do we stand?

The best method for citizens of the Third World to translate these contentious terms into language that First World visa officers would understand is to adapt one of Murphy's Laws: to get a visa, prove you don't need it.

Reza Baraheni

The Dream of the Man Who Could Not Go to Sleep

----

*"The aim of narrative is the transaction in the narrative,
not the appearance by which you can get rid of your boredom;
its aim is to dispel ignorance"[1] (Shams-e Tabrizi).*

That someone from abroad may have wanted me to take photos of some
of the paintings of Mozayyan, the Head Painter of the old Gajar dynasty
in the nineteenth century, or that I myself may have volunteered to take
them, should not change the fact that I am not a photographer. Everyone
is a photographer by accident, including me. But a real, professional
photographer is entirely a different species. His profession is not fishing. It is hunting, even though the two affairs may look similar to some
people. Catching a fish is fortuitous. Hunting is more premeditated, and
I prefer the hunter, but I do not advocate every act of his hunting. The
hunter's ability is of a quality you cannot dispense of so lightly. The
hunter shoots deliberately, as if he were shooting the final shot of the
firing squad. Well, let's move on.

I recently saw something very strange in Mathausen, a Nazi concentration camp. Some latter day European Nazis have denied the existence of the camp, and others have claimed that the inmates deserved
what they received.

It is three hours by car from Vienna. The road is utterly beautiful, and we drove out on a May day and arrived in Mathausen. There
were, in addition to Sanaz, my wife, and Arsalan, my small son, Behrouz

Heshmat, the sculptor from my hometown Tabriz, and Dr. Zjaleh Gohari, the United Nations physician, our wonderful host in Vienna. At first we took a tour of the statues and monuments built by different nations to honour the memory of their soldiers killed in Mathausen. They were all magnificent and as humane as they could be, and they became even more so after we visited the inside of the camp itself. The reality of the obnoxious face of Nazism and its reality-creating abilities could be seen more objectively by looking at the tools and instruments left behind in Mathausen's different buildings: remnants of a scrupulous science serving the ends of an equally scrupulous mass murder. A million people, perhaps even more than a million — men, women, and children — mostly of the so-called non-Aryan ethnic minorities, and a great number of Soviet prisoners of war, had been scientifically and systematically annihilated. Murder loses its atrocity when science is brought in to serve it. Although Nazism was not perhaps the first school to have had a scientific outlook towards systematic murder, there is no doubt that it gave the science unprecedented historical dimensions. Nazism considered murder a kind of scrupulous surgery and killed with such a level-headed precision that it seemed the skin, the flesh, the bones, the hearts, and the brains of human beings had been created for the sole purpose of promoting scientific research to the status of an enterprise serving the ends of murder.

Although one is utterly horrified, and racks one's brain asking why they have done this to humans, one cannot, however, help bowing, albeit in horror, before the ingenuity of the Nazi killers. One method in particular was much more flawless and bewildering than others. The prisoner would be hung from the ceiling of a small room. There was a hole in one of the walls, which the prisoner never noticed. A pistol aimed at the head of the prisoner from the hole. Everything was so flawless that there was no need to see the target. A hand pulled the trigger from the other side of the hole, and on this side the prisoner's brains went "bang" in an instant, like a popped balloon. As flawless as it could be. And this was the end. And I am not a photographer! And then it was the next person's turn. The pistol reloaded, the trigger, and then goodbye. And Serbs, a few hundred miles from Mathausen, inserted a skewer into the rectum of a six-year-old child, with the tip of the skewer thrust out of his mouth, and roasted him like a baby lamb before the very eyes of the child's mother, and then invited the mother to have a piece of the roasted meat. When she declined, they raped her and then shot her in the head. And Akbar Behkalam, our great painter in Berlin, has drawn a large poster of three men, with half of their faces of Turkish complexion and the second half Jewish, taken from a Jewish picture belonging to a poster of about fifty years ago. There are three men standing side by side, half Jewish, half Turkish, with an admonishing sentence on top of the poster: "We're the future Jews!" And the moral, economic, and racial crisis of Germany and all of Europe in general will soon blame everything on the non-Aryan ethnic groups. Not that Europe is a bad place, no, but half a million fathers have raped their daughters in Germany. Everyone was talking about it in Hamburg when I was on a reading tour in Germany about fourteen years ago. And I am not a photographer. Let us return to Vienna, say one or two things, and then move via Vienna to the north of Tehran. In one of the villages in the outskirts of Vienna, there is a place where Kafka had lived for some time, and there is an insane asylum — Dr. Gohari showed us from the top of the hills overlooking Vienna — where Kafka had lived towards the end of his days. And there is always a "K" in Europe, haunting everywhere, and taking flawless pictures. And I am not a photographer.

And Vienna moves in the mind of the poet like waves, with the nocturnal glory of operatic voices from the catacombs, and the barrels and the tall overflowing chalices of its beer and wine. And Freud's home, and the home of psychoanalysis, and Breughel's works are all here. And Heshmat explains the museums. And the city? No one has ever said or written that Vienna was not beautiful. No Mauthausen anywhere around here. If you distribute the statues among the population, each inhabitant will carry home a dozen of them. They are everywhere. And watching the top of some of the magnificent cathedrals you have to be careful, you will break your neck. And Heshmat is taking pictures all the time. Mozart, Beethoven, and the statues, and one is afraid that they might willfully hurl themselves down from their towering height of four or five hundred feet.

One of the purest and most modern spirits of my hometown is this Behrouz Heshmat. And in the middle of one of our nights in Vienna, we pay a visit to a huge iron statue of his in a thoroughly lit park. (And I don't know how the censorship could think of hiding his statue, portraying the personality of *Ashigh,* the folk musician of the Azeri nationality in Iran, behind the walls of the Tabriz Museum in Iran, like a bouquet of fresh roses tossed on a dunghill!) And another specimen of such unique spirits is Zhaleh Gohari, a gem, hidden in Vienna — like the scores of an unknown piano concerto by Mozart or Beethoven hidden in the folds of a book, to be discovered and performed later by the exhilarating orchestra of a sudden discovery: ("I am not one of those guys who goes out of his way to welcome someone. If he gets angry and runs away, I will run away a hundred times over. God greets me ten times, and I don't greet back. Then I say '[greetings] back to you ten times over,' and pretend I am deaf. Now you stand there and watch. Get angry, and watch me how I get back to you in my anger.")[2] And I am not a photographer. And in taking a really good picture, I see some resemblance to that shot from the hidden hole towards and into the brains, as if somewhere the scrupulous crime, political murder, and genocide corresponded with very scrupulously performed works of art. When the human mind operates meticulously and with concentration, it performs a surgical operation, creates laser beams, produces the beautiful poem "The Long-legged Fly" of W.B.Yeats; where Michelangelo's hand, Julius Caesar's mind, and the lover's heart all work equally scrupulously; or turns into the harmonious and meticulous eye so that it will take a picture of the hand, the eye, the colour, and the hundred-year-old figural concordances of Mozaayan, the Head Painter of the fruit inside the glasses. To take a picture for a friend in need of the picture in the United States. And I am not a photographer!

My photographer is Faramarz Soleimani, who gave me two of the pictures he took, which I sent to the person who had asked for them, and now I don't have copies of them. And he told me, when he was giving me the pictures, to tell my party in the U.S. to put on record who the photographer was. I don't know who is going to do that. I am going on record myself now. Maybe the pictures were printed somewhere. This has always been the case with this world. One mental cubism is criminal; the second an artistic metonymy, parallel to the first one; the third is an eye in sleep, the radiation of destruction. And the caller from the U.S. says: "They say the paintings are in the possession of someone by the name of Dr. Saghafi, who is interested in memoirs, paintings, and pictures; and in ghosts, spiritism, séance, and archetypes arising from the spirit of religious revelations." And I — interested in all things contradictory and antithetical: Theodor Adorno, Walter Benjamin, André Breton, Faulkner, Joyce, Jung, Kurosawa, the Aztec art, galactic airfields of Central America's pre-Colombian mountaintops (unless Von Daniken had lied), observatories of humanity's childhood, Ezekiel and John's Revelations, the physical, spiritual, and linguistic ascensions, the ever-flowing intelligence of Nima Youshij, the founder of modern Persian poetry, and the innocent early years of Forough Farrokhzad, Iran's first great woman poet — feel captivated by this Dr. Saghafi.

And all of these hurl my psychological disharmony into a world made of flooding streams, wherein I see the artist as the dejected spy of the Nimaian or non-Nimaian melancholy, with relishes from Freud and Mossaddegh,[3] with the mouth and jaw cancers of both of them, and particularly a picture of Mossaddegh facing the desert with a stick in his hand and his back to the hidden camera of history. And good heavens! Should not this memory of mine be stoned to death! Because the son of a bitch is like a hand with its stubby thumb always getting stuck in a hole; as simple as that; and then the other fingers turn around it like imagination's whirligigs, with a destructive sense of centripetality, such as the whirling heads of the "Spirit's Kurd" of Haji-Sadegh, the Jeylani dervish,[4] like Ali Dehbashi's[5] thick and voluminous telephone book, in which all the names of literary humans and jinn ("Which then of the bounties of thine Lord will thee deny?")[6] whirl around incessantly, providing guidance like a computer; like the painful memory I have had of Hossein Mansour al-Hallaj; like the southern Tehran, with its ancient deteriorating ghettoes, the Arab Neighbourhood, Yaftabad, Yakhchiabad and the rest, which now reveal their poverty and their ruination more forcefully as a consequence of half-built parks by Mayor Karbaschi, with alleys, roads, and fountains overlooking the poor, ruined houses in the ghettos. From their depths, the eyes of young boys and girls in daytime and the twinkling of cats' eyes from the darkness of night cut through this world, and a human being is nothing but the distorted memory of places and times, of escapes and returns, and of rest and restlessness (and I will be quite ready to give up my spirit but not the restlessness of my spirit). And I have been in contact with the greatest souls of the world, I have phoned Hermes, Dionysus, Shams-e Tabrizi, and the Old Man of the Magi,[7] and I have written a *Book of Kings* based on the souls of the Omm-al-Sebyan[8] in the Persian Gulf, and in the symbolical language of the tortured spirits of the dethroned Shamans of Central Asia walking in their tattered clothes, to the background of the geography of an Internal North, sucked into the depths of Aryan plateaus. And this time, that central thumb was the name of Dr. Saghafi; and around him danced my other fingers, my pens turned around like whirligigs; because history is always my prehistory; and it is I who is history in the moment of the becoming of the horizons; a present tense made of millions of presences, speeches, discourses, moaning, and bemoaning; such as the concentric music of circles in the cross-section of the tall trees, the five hundred-year-old oriental, Anis-al-doleh plane trees of Dr. Saghafi's house; with the concrete poetry of the stable but dancing images, dancing in place; and the poetry of the whole past of Iran and the world is the pre-poetry of my poetry, the poetry of all the I's of my I; and you, all Iranian poets!, arise on the central circles of the penta-textured, fish-marked silk carpets of Tabriz and Khoy[9] and the pre-Jungian, pre-Western mandalas so that we will dance to the rhythm of the pre-renaissance music that sounds like our own music, and the improvisations of John Cage and the blind internal vision of the drumming of the drummer Tehrani; a dancing with presence, with feet raised above the earth, an imaginary earth, a space made of the architecture of the abstraction of the souls and the psyche: Dr. Saghafi, rayray, rayray/weeps night and day, hayhay, hayhay — My fever is of the fever of Tehrani/ you stay with me, naynay, naynay (nay = flute)/ Dr. Saghafi, ayay, ayay, ayay/ Hananaa, hoohoo, hananaa, hayhay—give me that may, that may, that may/ maymay, maymay, may-may, maymay (may = wine).

And finally I found out where the two paintings were, who Dr. Saghafi was, and started asking everyone, and I even found a book Dr. Saghafi had translated by Alexander Dumas forty or fifty years earlier, long before Zabih-ol-lah Mansouri, Dumas's famous translator, translated anything by Dumas into Persian. And I found the book in one of the cellars of an underground bookstore in Tehran. I did not read it. I sent it to the person who had wanted the pictures from the paintings by Mozaayan, the Head Painter. And I am not a photographer. And in those days Dr. Faramarz Soleimani had not come up with the idea of turning himself into the leader of the Third Wave of Persian poetry; and questioning here and there, I found out that he was a very capable photographer; and when I got hold of Dr. Saghafi's number, I dialled it, and how kind, how polite he was, and what a fine speaker on the phone, and how cultured. He said: "You will come up to the large gate of the Niyavaran Palace, the former Sahebgharaniyeh palace, and you will come up the stairs right across from the palace. You will see two plane trees. Our home is right across from the plane trees. In fact the plane trees belong to us." "But Dr. Saghafi, there are so many plane trees around. How can we say which is yours!" He said: "No, these plane trees aren't ordinary ones. You won't miss them. I'll be at your service here. I have the paintings, and you can take as many pictures as you wish. Goodbye."

And we went there.

At first I had thought of taking a book, a collection of poetry or a bouquet of flowers for Dr. Saghafi, but I don't know what happened to my mind. I forgot all about it and went there without carrying anything. Dr. Soleimani was there already, fully equipped, top-notch, cool, and polite. There were so many tools hanging from every side of him that it seemed we were going to the Majnoun Islands of the Iran-Iraq war to make a documentary. If you plant Soleimani's face on a miniature of Saedi's[10] head, you will get the magical realist face of Gabriel García Márquez at the moment he had finished the writing of "The Incredible and Sad Tale of Innocent Erendira and Her Heartless Grandmother." The fact is that we are always being submerged in magic and we are not aware of it, and in the couple of hours of the sunset of the Niyavaran quarter on the North of Tehran, everything was steeped in magic.

When we went up the stairs, there was not a building to be seen, or at least we did not see any. I didn't know how Soleimani felt, but all of a sudden, I stopped breathing because I came to realize why Dr. Saghafi had spoken of the plane trees on the phone: "The plane trees are ours!" Of course, later, I recognized that the trees did not belong to anyone. Two heavy-set ghouls belonging to *The Thousand and One Nights*, resembling two awesome brick-kilns, with the leaves and branches of their tops swarming with birds and mounting to touch the sky. I don't know why I was reminded of Rustam, the hero of *The Book of Kings*, the Persian epic by Ferdowsi. So, this was what it meant, "The plane trees are ours," in a flat backyard of no more than two or three thousand metres. And I thought that if somebody kept time, I, who had no cholesterol, had no addiction to anything, and had fine lungs, could run around one of these poplars in about thirty seconds. Bewildered, we went ahead and, up there on top of the trees, there was the chaotic sound of the birds, the hidden birds. No doubt these birds had startled the Shah of Iran from sleep, and before him Ahmad Shah, Mozaffar-al-din Shah, Nasser-al-din Shah — but not Reza Shah,[11] because he never slept in this palace — or perhaps lulled them to sleep. (If one is not a king, how can he understand anything of the relation of kings to birds on top of four to five hundred-year-old plane trees? I will know when I become king and will let you know.) And it was natural for the two of us to try and find out. And we went ahead, but we did not see anyone. It seemed that the garden and the plane trees had been leased to ghosts. Only a few steps away from one of the busiest northern streets of Tehran during the rush hour, right on the corner across from the Niavaran palace, where the street took a turn to the north, Dr. Soleimani and I, "two lonely, two homeless, two desolate people,"[12] walked in this silence-ridden no-man's land, and it seemed that once in distant times in the past Abel and Cain had walked on this land, and that first catastrophe, the slaying of one brother by the other, the first man born on earth a murderer, and the second his victim, had taken place. And when the man had straightened his back and stood up, he had killed his own brother by his side, and then protested: "Am I my brother's keeper?"

Perhaps the reason we felt ourselves in a desert was that the plane trees were so tall. They were so tall that the house on the other side looked really low, physically, objectively. It seemed not to exist. Like the small figure of the late Akhavane Sales[13] against that huge accursed rock of his poem or in contrast to the majesty of his words: "This ill-ruled, insane century!" or before Bahram's cave in "The Story of the City of Stones."[14] Compared with the plane trees, the house looked like a house for Pinocchio. And it was not unlike the legacy home of my own childhood in the "Mortuary Ghetto" of Tabriz, only a few sizes larger, more spread out, much cleaner, and as Nima had said, "less broken." But Nima's curse had at least been answered in this particular case.

And the people say:
"more broken be the gates of their gardens!
and more crouched be each of them, separated from his family
at the platform of his door!
and from the songs of their death, quenched be upon
the ceilings of their balconies, their chandeliers!"
"yes, let it be quenched!" a distant voice says
and another voice nearby
in the tumult of voices reaching the road, says:
"let this be their deserved punishment
at the end of their periods of joy
after their ages of rapture!"[15]

I don't know why Dr. Soleimani did not walk ahead of me. I thought it was out of courtesy. The house had a middle section with two flanks. This much for my knowledge of architecture! I cannot describe architecture. I enjoy it without being able to describe it. As a result, I don't know how to describe anything. I know how to narrate, but I don't know description. The place plus the person who is in that place, plus I, who perceive the person in that place, make that thing that I call narrative. Consequently, I speak with everyone, but when there is no one anywhere, I fill the place in my mind with human beings, otherwise I won't be able to speak about it. We were near the left flank, the Western side. A door was open. I looked inside. A sixty- or seventy-year-old woman sat there, almost in the dark. My eyes were not accustomed to the darkness yet. It seemed as though all the birds on top of the plane trees sat on my nose; like the bird on the face of the René Magritte painting I used to love sometime ago and now I even loved more. There were not lights in the room. So, where did the light come from? I was reminded of Madam Sosostris of Eliot's "The Waste Land" with her evil pack of cards; and then reminded of Ezra Pound's "Portrait d'une Femme" and "The Portrait of a Lady" by Eliot; but was not reminded of "The Portrait of a Lady" by myself.

Around the women of both portraits of the two poets, old bourgeois-aristocratic paraphernalia could be seen. I had sensed that there must be similar things around this woman, too. Of course, you were not supposed to look at a woman's face in the Islamic Iran, but here you could not help it. It was an accident. You cannot stop a sudden look! And I have seen a great many depressed women. She had her hands on the table. She looked nervous. I did not know who she was. She wore old but respectable clothes. She had a rather wide but haggard face. The cards were sprawled on the table, and I told you that the hands were on the table too. And she kept looking at the distance between the hands and the cards. Behind her was completely dark, but strange ghosts could be discerned in the background. It seemed that a number of huge elephants had been tied to a manger, with their backs to the woman's back and towards my face. As if in the Museum of Modern Art in New York the lights had gone out, and the lights around the big works were also out, and the spectators had all shut their eyes and were silent, with some of them leaning on their retirement clubs and watching the insides of their fallen eyelids, and behind the eyelids the world rolled this way and that way. I asked the woman: "Excuse me, Dr. Saghafi's home?" She did not even so much as raise her head to me. The polite Dr. Soleimani, "Our Titan of the Cameras," had arrived now at the window. I became more polite, more tender, slow and slow, like the poetry of one of my favourite poets, Gertrude Stein:

> *Kiss my lips. She did.*
> *Kiss my lips again she did.*
> *Kiss my lips over and over and over again she did.*
> *I have feathers.*
> *Gentle fishes.*[16]

Once more I asked her: "Dr. Saghafi's home?" I had never been so lyrical in my life. She lifted her arm, the left one, and snapped: "In that room!" I was reminded of the story of the slave of Kavoos Voshmgir in *Ghabousnameh*, who, upon hearing his master order him: "Turn your ass to me," had said, "Master, you could say this in better words." "How?" the master asked. The slave said: "You could have said, turn your face to the other side."

And when I turned back, I immediately regretted it. She was watching us. Was she also rotting in there like the T.S. Eliot's aristocracy in "The Waste Land"? Had she also fallen with the fall of the Shah? Had her horse's leg been broken? And now, we could be her fancy, departing. As we moved away now, we did not know whether she was watching us. To tell you the truth, I did not have the courage to turn back and look. I had already come to the conclusion that Dr. Soleimani, too, was scared like me. Now the two of us walked as if trekking in the pre-Colombian Amazon jungles. And everything seemed to be new, strange, and frightful now.

We arrived at the door of the right flank. I knocked with the backs of my fingers. Silence. Dr. Soleimani and I exchanged the only meaningful look we had exchanged in our lives. He plucked up courage and turned his head to the right and looked. It seemed as though the silence after the knocking of the door had caught up with the birds on the treetops. Dr. Soleimani turned his head to its original position. And at this moment I came to realize something I had not realized before: The birds had been watching us all along. The diagram of their relations with each other changed with our movements here on the ground. They drew the diagram of our instincts on the sky with their sounds. And between the door and the silence of the landlord of the house, there had come into existence a meaningful, or perhaps a polysemous, relationship. The commander of the birds was behind the door. Whenever he breathed, the diagram of the singing of birds started. And now he had temporarily emitted his soul from his body and sent it out into other bodies. That was why it was silent everywhere and the voice would start only when he would summon his soul, with the magnet of his body from all other bodies, times, and places.

But before he did that, let me say a few words about myself:

In such moments, when I am waiting and I want something to happen to save me from the purgatory in which I am stuck, I am reminded of things that are generally evil, terrible, and beautiful. The Lame Tamerlain, when all broken and defeated and seated with his back to a wall, had learned from an ant that had climbed the opposite wall seventy times and fallen, how to pluck up courage again, regain his strength, and start to kill and build hillocks of beheaded men and women. This was the lesson we were taught as children at school on "the will to power." Of course, this is not what I am reminded of now. Here is the problem: In these moments of anticipation, first of all, I become extremely lonely; second, I can simply continue and go up to nine or twelve, and I don't go on and go up. And instead, I am reminded of something that has nothing to do with things going around me: I am reminded now of the last poem the French poet Robert Desnos wrote, the most lyrical of all poems of the world in the Nazi concentration camp, addressed to his beloved, who was none other than his own wife; and how happy is the man who upon death has his wife and lover gathered together in one person, the same person.

> *I've dreamed of you so much that you have lost your reality ...*
> *Oh equilibriums of the emotional scales! ...*
> *I've dreamed of you so much, walked and talked so much*
> *And slept so much with your phantom presence*
> *That all I can do now, and perhaps all I can go on doing now*
> *Is to remain a phantom among phantoms*
> *A shadow, a hundred times more shadowy than that shape*
> *moving now*
> *And which will go on moving,*
> *Stepping lightly across the sundial of your life.*[17]

I want to scream and say that I want none of this. The hell with Mozaayan, the Head Painter, the paintings, and the pictures! And now the door opens, and a tall, respectable man of about seventy-five or eighty, in a perfect suit with a tie and a shirt and shoes to match, appears at the door and says: "Hello, Doctor! Come on in." I turn to Dr. Soleimani: "Doctor, after you." And then Dr. Saghafi tells Dr. Soleimani: "Hello, Doctor, please come in." With the repetition of these compliments, all the spirits who had been summoned up to the stage because of our fears, retreat to their hidden, abstract groves.

The world becomes normal again. However, Dr. Saghafi is so neat and top-notch, so perfect and poised, that I feel he must have combed and brushed his hair, brushed also the shoulders of his jacket and shined his shoes to prepare himself to appear before us. And when we go in, it strikes me for a second that I should ask him whether it was true that his spirit had left his body temporarily, and that it was back now, re-entering him only for our sake. And if not so, then we must have been dreaming or imagining all along. But I give up asking questions, because he is at that very moment explaining that he had bought the paintings of the Head Painter from his inheritors, two brothers, both generals of the Shah's regime, one of them among the conspirators who killed Afshar-Tous, Premier Mossadegh's chief of police, and the other, a general at the Shah's own service. And it seemed that he didn't remember whether they had been given to his father as a present by the two generals' father or they themselves had given them to Dr. Saghafi as presents. And the Head Painter was really the Head Painter, the teacher of even the Master Kamal-al-molk,[18] and like the Master had gone to Europe, had copied the works of the European masters, and these two paintings might also be copies. I don't know. That is to say, he didn't know. And Soleimani is looking for the electricity outlet to have more light for the pictures he will be taking. The atmosphere always needs more light. And Dr. Saghafi, when showing the outlet, points on the wall of the upper part of the room to a picture in which Mozaffar-al-din Shah is resting in a garden with the same dreamy eyes of Ali Nassirian, the actor, and Ali Hatami, the director of the film dealing with the Shah; and there is a rather fat man, i.e., the father of Dr. Saghafi, A'lam-al-dowleh, who has extended his hand in fear and trembling, holding a paper towards the ailing Shah, and it seems that the Shah is quite prepared to sign it. And exactly at the moment when the Shah is bidding beads to see whether he should sign the Imperial Firman or not, exactly at the historical moment of this explanation or the historical moment of the signing of the Firman, the lights go out and the room is delivered to absolute darkness.

What can we do now? Everything stays alone and dark. Dr. Saghafi, Dr. Soleimani, Dr. Baraheni, Kamal-al-molk, the Head Painter, the paintings, the signature of the Firman of the Constitution. Everything and everyone stays alone and in the dark. Only the tongueless whisper of world's spirits can be heard coming down the plane trees and the walls, walking upside down on the ceiling and licking the paintings, with the grease from their tongues tarnishing the paintings. Groping our way through, with Dr. Saghafi in front followed by the two other doctors, one of them a gynecologist, the other a doctor of language and literature, we come out of the room. Outside it is light, it is beautiful, it is an hour before the sunset. The birds are singing. Dr. Soleimani is taking pictures. Dr. Saghafi tells us that each plane tree is four or five hundred years old, and that whenever Mohammad-Reza [he means the deposed Shah of Iran] came out of the castle in his car, he would order the driver to stop the car and then he would get out, look at the plane trees, and pay his tribute to the trees because he thought they held good omens for him, then he would get in the car and go after his business; and perhaps on the last day he left the castle, he had not come out of the car to pay his tribute to the trees, and consequently, had faced the calamities that culminated with his death.

For a split second it passed through my mind that had I been the Shah, instead of running away from Iran on that last day, I would have gone up one of the plane trees and would have sat there on the top, by or inside the tumultuous nests of the birds, and would not have cared to come down, even if not one but a hundred revolutions were to take place. And we went and stood by the trees and took pictures, first Dr. Soleimani of Dr. Saghafi and me, and then I of Dr. Saghafi and Dr. Soleimani, and then Dr. Saghafi of the two of us. And then we stopped taking pictures, and we talked, not of the spirits, of painting, of the Head Painter, or of the woman who probably sat still there in the room at the table, with the spirits of elephants behind her back, controlling their urge to sneeze. Instead we talked of the setting of the sun that was approaching, and it was the largest orange of the firmaments that was rising upon us, rather than setting; yes, it was rising; and then suddenly it went away, and almost as suddenly, everywhere was lit in a different way, and we felt the light. It was the electricity that had come back. We went into one of the rooms in the middle of the building between the two flanks. There were cardboard boxes on the floor by the walls: "These are all manuscripts," Dr. Saghafi said, "Very precious ones. And this room, you know, is the chamber of Anis-al-doleh, the most favourite wife of Nasser-al-din Shah. This building used to be Anis-al-doleh's palace, which belongs to us now, and these tiles here are the tiles of the same palace."

>*the day*
>*passed on tiptoe*
>*through the burning spears of silver*
>>*in the most slanted shadow*
>*so that years later*
>*it will give the repetition of Blue*
>>*amorously*
>*a meaning of home (country)*
>
>*the siesta's vaults, the vaulted siesta*
>*and the sleepy whisper of a hesitant fountain*
>*on the silence of the thirsting petunias*
>*and the unbelieving repetition of thousands of bitter almonds*
>*on a thousand sexangular mirrors of tiles*
>*years later*
>*years later*
>>*on a warm midday*
>>>*suddenly*
>*distant memory of the closed home pool*
>
>>>*O, the prince of tiles*
>>>*with those blue tears!*[19]

And how do we solve the problem of time in this poem for ourselves, for the poem, for the poet, for the poet of this poem who is no longer Shamlou, but me, Dr. Soleimani, or Dr. Saghafi? We cannot divide it into its parts. It exists as a whole. We perceive its existence. We have been taken by surprise by the objects of other times. The objects of our times have taken those objects by surprise. We possess lost throats. We contact the lost continents of time. Words are our contacts. They point to those hidden worlds. The electricity that had gone comes back, lights a part of the world, and then goes out. Only Iranians can understand the "repetition of Blue" alluding to "the meaning of home (country)." The Shah hides in our being. He goes away. We go away, and the "prince of tiles" is awakened in the "thousand sexangular mirrors of tiles." We move in time spaces, through the seemingly trivial screws and bolts of language. The problem is this: I am standing on these tiles. The plane trees are older than Tehran, and the tiles, the meaning of the tiles, are older than the plane trees, and they suggest a meaning of home (country) to my mind, and Anis-al-doleh becomes the woman sitting in the elephant-coloured room, bent on her cards for her fortune. No lyrical poem returns to the man or the woman about whom the poem was written. If it did, it would be prose, not poetry. The poem with the whole sum of its personalities and images moves beyond each particle in the process of leaving behind its particularity, to express a completeness that is only the completeness of that particular poem. Thus all the good poems of the world are lyrical, because a lyrical poem is a poem in which all words have fallen in love with each other, like the lovers themselves, to a degree that they (the words) have become inseparable.

"If you don't mind, Dr. Saghafi, we will go to the room with the paintings and take our pictures."

And we go back and take pictures. Dr. Soleimani is taking the pictures, and very professionally. And I watch the serene and dignified face of this young man of seventy-five or seventy-six years old, always wanting to ask him to invoke for us the spirits attributed to our world. He no longer speaks. I get up, and he gets up. And he tells us the way we should get back, so that we won't get lost. We leave behind us Saghafi, the woman, the tiles, Anis-al-doleh, Mozaayan, the Head Painter, and those two pre-historical plane trees on Tehran's shoulder. We walk into the street. Dr. Soleimani asks me: "Are you going to write about it?" — "I don't know, I might," I say. And now, have I written the story of our visit to Dr. Saghafi's place or the adventures of my visit to the world inside myself reflected in labyrinthine mirrors?

And some time later, it seems as if the question I wanted to ask Dr. Saghafi in connection with ghosts attributed to the world, visit me in a dream, not in a detailed and extended pattern, but in a selected, laconic form, the way things appear to you in a poem. I wrote the poem immediately after I woke up. A question is the answer to the answer. And the answer does not exist. I only ask the questions. Read these words by Jean Jacques Rousseau, before you read the poem:

The dreams of a bad night are given to us in philosophy. You will
say I too am a dreamer; I admit it, but I do what others fail to do,
and I give my dreams as dreams, and leave the reader to discover
whether there is anything in them which may prove useful to those
who are awake.[20]

It Seems That Even the Dream Is Not the Same Dream

when I leaped from the sun to the shade, I saw that the shade was not my
shade
returning
I saw that the sun was not the same sun
on the margins of the sun and the shade
I saw both 550-year-old plane trees of Anis-al-doleh
                                    turning round the woman at whirlpool speed
and the woman screamed behind the leaves
with no one to dispel the ghosts of Saghafi's house
from behind the paintings of Mozaayan, the Head Painter,
blue termites had crept out from underneath the 100-year-old tiles
going up the books of dreams, ghosts and fantasies
and there were no birds
and the woman screamed from behind the leaves
I saw the Shah standing outside the castle
holding hands with a trembling witch
watching both the 550-year-old plane trees belonging to Saghafi
the Hour is all the hours   the Hour is all the hours   the Hour is all the
hours
arms crossed, helpless and disturbed
old and dead men of several millennia ago stood in line
                                    on the margins of a 550 year old silk carpet
and the silk square was spouting all its colours up to the circular air
a visionary space rained down from the colours.

when I tell the dream I see that it is not the same dream
when I leaped from the sun to the shade, I saw that the shade was not
my shade
returning
I saw that the sun was not the same sun
the Seer is gone, the Hour is all the hours, only a space of
vision remains[21]

A NOTE ON THE TEXT

This article and poem were reprinted in Reza Baraheni, *The Vigilant Vision* (A Collection of Essays on The Theory of Writing and Reading of the Literary Text) in 1974, but it was not allowed to be distributed by the Censorship Bureau of the Ministry of Islamic Culture and Guidance until 1999. The attached poem at the end of the article was included in Reza Baraheni, *Accosting the Butterflies* (Tehran, Markaz Publishing House, 1994), the poet's last collection of poetry before he was forced to leave Iran in 1996, and sought asylum in Canada in January 1997 with his family. "The Vigilant Vision," the original title of the present essay, lent its name to the entire book by that title. The Persian version has been printed several times in the Persian periodicals of the Iranian Diaspora, including *Shahrvand* of Toronto, Canada. A French translation of the essay is under way.

The English translation and the footnotes to the translation belong to Reza Baraheni himself.

1   Mohammad Shams-e Tabrizi, *The Essays*, Mohammad-Ali Movahhed (ed.) (Tehran, Kharazmi Publications, 1970), 273.

2   Ibid., 273.

3   Mohammad Mossadegh, Iran's democratically elected prime minister, ousted by the CIA coup in 1953.

4   Abd-al-ghader Jeylani, the founder of the Ghaderi sect of Kurdish Dervishes in Iran, Hadji-Sadegh (Sadeghi) is the contemporary leader of the sect.

5   Ali Dehbashi, editor of first *Kelk* and later *Bokhara* periodicals, two contemporary periodicals in Iran.

6   The refrain verse in the Al-rahman chapter of the *Qur'an*, tr. M.H. Shakir (Elmhurst, New York, Tahrike Tarsile Qur'an, Inc., 1997), 533. I have edited the translation slightly.

7   An imaginary character in the poetry of the classical mystical Persian poet, Hafez, who acted as his source of inspiration.

8   It is an Arabic word, originally made of two words, and it means literally, the mother of children born with epilepsy or spasm. But when in the southern ports of Iran, a person is supposed to have been stricken by Omm-al-Sebyan, pronounced in the area as Ommossebyan, it means that he is mentally sick, because the demon has stricken him. The blame on the mother may have been because of the dominance of patriarchy.

9   Two cities in the Azerbaijam province of Iran, famous for the patterns of their rugs, particularly those of Tabriz.

10   Gholam-Hossein Saedi, one of Iran's prominent playwrights and fiction writers of the Pahlavi period (1936–1965).

11   The first three were kings of the Gajar dynasty that ruled Iran before Reza Shah Pahlavi ended their rule and placed himself on the throne. His son, Mohammad-Reza, was deposed by the revolution of 1979.

12   A half-line of poetry from Hafez.

13   A famous half-classical, half modern poet of the second half of the twentieth century of Iran.

14   Bahram, a half-legendary and half historical pre-Islamic Iranian king, who disappeared at the end of his life in a cave, and Akhavane Sales's narrative poem is the mythical story of his death.

15   *Yadollah Jalali Pendari*, Nima Youshidj (ed.) (Tehran, Morvarid, 1991), 167–8.

16   Gertrude Stein, *The Yale Gertrude Stein*, Selections with an Introduction by Richard Kostelanetz (New Haven and London, Yale University Press, 1980), 19–20.

17   Quoted here in a shortened form from Michael Benedikt, *The Poetry of Surrealism* (Boston, Toronto, Little, Brown and Company, 1974), 268.

18   Iran's chief painter of the Realist school at the end of the nineteenth century and early decades of the twentieth century.

19   Ahmad Shamlou, *She're Zamane Ma*, with analysis and interpretation by Mohammad Hoghoughi, (Tehran, Zamane Ma Publishing House, 1982), 292–3.

20   Quoted from Rousseau's *Émile* in Jacques Derrida's *Of Grammatology*, (The Johns Hopkins University Press, Baltimore, 1976), 316.

21   Note on the publication history of the essay and the poem: The essay, including the poem at the end, was first published in a collection by the editor and architect, Sima Kooban, in *Ketabe Tehran* (*The Book of Tehran*), a collection of articles and pictures, by Iranian writers, artists and architects on the city of Tehran, in 1992.

Faruk Myrtaj

How I Discovered Canada Through its Literature

Many things about Canada remain unknown in my country, tiny Albania, yet most of what is known derives from literature. Margaret Atwood, Alice Munro, and a few other writers are recognized, but mainly only by their names alone or in books concerning Albanians. In any case, such names are only a fragment in the great mosaic of Canada's literature.

By contrast, American literature is much more conspicuous in Albania, and many American writers are well known there. Although no one can deny their writing abilities, I am sure that U.S. dominance in the world is one important factor in the global acceptance of its literature. It's a literary superpower!

If Canadian writers feel neglected, they should know that the writers of Albania have it worse. Their language is also limited in its reach. Although Albanian is one of the oldest languages in Europe, it is read and spoken by relatively few people. By contrast, English Canadian writers communicate in the most widespread and influential language in the world. Communicating in such a language, everything is possible: readers, money, fame. Of course, the fact remains that literature is always literature in whatever language it is written.

In the early 1990s, I worked for the Albanian Ministry of Culture. At that time, the House of the Albanian Book gave us some issues of the Canadian literary magazine *Exile*. In *Exile* I found poems, short stories, interviews, and dialogues that immediately attracted my curiosity. This was my first taste of original Canadian literature. Because of the satisfaction the *Exile* pieces gave me, and wanting to share it, I decided to translate some of them. I also thought that it would be a good challenge to translate from English. At that time I had never thought about emigrating — though of course it is practically impossible to predict the forces that drive us in our lives.

I translated a short story by Barry Callaghan called "The Black Queen" and sent it to a newspaper. The main character is part of a modern couple, a couple that happens to be not a man and a woman but a man and a man. The editor of the newspaper wasn't ready to publish the story: "I would not like to have this character in my cultural supplement ...." he told me.

I was conscious that the characters in Callaghan's story were unusual in some ways, but I didn't expect such intolerance from the editor as he was considered a talented writer in my country. ("The Black Queen" was published later in another newspaper.) Thus, not only had I started discovering Canada by reading and translating its literature, but at the same time I began to realize some truths about my own society — its readers and its writers.

Later I translated an essay by Robert Zend concerning the originality and authenticity of various internationally famous authors, with graphic representations of their creations. The marvellous conversation between J. L. Borges and Robert Zend was published in *Drita*, the newspaper of the Albanian Writers' Association. As Zend and Borges make clear, creation is collective. Everyone adds something to it: the author, his friends, the publisher, the readers, and so on. In this way, all the books have already been written and we may find them in the "World Library." Newly written books only serve to change the way we read and understand previously written ones. Back then in Albania, this way of thinking was not widespread. But this article interested many people.

From Matt Cohen's work I translated the short story "The Eiffel Tower in Three Parts." Again, the subject was irritating for readers who were used to socialist literature. How was it possible that the father of a girl would offer his daughter to a man? However, this short story still got published before "The Black Queen." At least Cohen's story featured a conventional couple: a man and a woman.

In another issue of *Exile* I found a short story extracted from Leon Rooke's *Shakespeare's Dog*. In Rooke's story, a young girl tries to get the body of her dead lover through customs without paying a too hefty bribe: money remains important for the living. The writer doesn't attempt to cover up this cold, hard reality. It would have been difficult to find an Albanian writer who could afford to write so honestly.

– – – – –

In 1999, I completed my translation of William Saroyan's *Selected Stories*, a task I undertook only for my pleasure, not as an obligation. Therefore, I took my time in finishing it. Saroyan's Armenia was depicted as a proud, strong country, and the author apparently felt empathy towards people, Armenian or not. Because I fear that modern society and its literature are losing this much-needed humanity, I liked Saroyan's characters.

Three years later, an Albanian publisher made me an offer to translate Alistair MacLeod's novel *No Great Mischief*. I accepted immediately. I didn't know what kind of a writer Alistair MacLeod was, but my acquaintance with Canadian literature made me think that I'd enjoy it. It's a great pleasure to encounter another writer with the same nature and opinions as one's own, and this is how I felt about Alistair MacLeod. Though it wasn't easy to do, translating *No Great Mischief* was a great experience and taught me more about Canadian culture. MacLeod's characters, mainly Scottish immigrants, had much in common with Albanian highlanders and their traditions. In one unforgettable scene a photographer must stand far away from his subjects so that everyone can be included in a family photograph. Large families with a lot of children, grandchildren, dogs, and cats like the one portrayed in the novel are traditional in Albania.

There is another reason I enjoyed reading and translating this novel. Before attending university, I had worked as a coal miner for five years, which made me agree, just this once, with what Vladimir Lenin said: "The mistreatment of man by man will exist as long as underground work exists." I realized that the lives of coal miners are the same in every country, from east to west, just as human beings are the same everywhere. The best part of *No Great Mischief* comes when the author describes a miner's life, his suffering, and his encounters with death. I had seen these things with my own eyes, witnessed my co-workers in the same difficulties, had been one of them. I saw them buried under rocks; drank with them in bars stinking of alcohol to forget the dangers; and made the workers characters of my own short stories. I have a photograph of all of us together. Circled in dark red are the people who were killed underground.

No Great Mischief provides some striking descriptions of Canadian nature, and the ice fishing is especially memorable. The transportation of people across the freezing water is unforgettable, too, as in the depiction of people's love for each other. By reading these kinds of books, Albanians form positive views of Canada. I am sure that some of MacLeod's readers thought of coming to Canada either as visitors or as immigrants.

Around this time, my family and I decided to move to Canada to make a better life for ourselves. Yet, although I was highly critical of what was happening at home, I was extremely reluctant to leave my country. I was a journalist, and my real value was in my own language. I had heard in a thousand ways that it was impossible to become a writer in another language and culture, but I had also heard that Canada was multicultural. Every day, I discovered new facets of what was to become my new home. Around this time, I was given a copy of the *Oxford Book of Canadian Short Stories*, an anthology edited by Margaret Atwood and Robert Weaver. Reading it, I became convinced that Canada suited me. I admired the fact that Canadian citizens appeared to be polite and helpful. But there were too many pros and cons. I spent much time learning about and preparing for Canada but also trying to resist emigration. I was not just discovering Canada, I was discovering myself. I was hesitant. I had been talking with relatives, friends, and colleagues about my distaste for emigration, while, at the same time, I was becoming comfortable in the Canadian environment by reading the anthology.

However, when I saw the contributors' birthdates in the anthology, I noticed that young writers appeared rarely: the situation was the same in Albania. But I knew that age is one thing and literature is another. Life changes and writers' skills improve. Canada was progressing in its development, and its literature was also evolving. I would become part of this transformation. I then learned that two of the authors I had translated had died. I never had a chance to meet or know them personally, but I had loved their creations and their ideas. This was more than enough reason to feel good in this country. In my application to the Writers' Union of Canada, I wrote, "I have my dead people here." Canada had already begun to feel like home.

Through its literature, I discovered Canada and at the same time I began to understand myself much better, away from my homeland, with my guard down. This is translation: leaving from somewhere, going somewhere else. Literature reaches far and wide; it is not only Canadian, or American, or French, or even Albanian. I believe that literature is everywhere, with no boundaries. It is the ultimate discovery.

Martha Kumsa

Without Charge or Trial: Ten Years in a Canadian Prison

I stare into the dark, half asleep, half awake. Is it just a nightmare? Can I wake up and shake it off? I want to scream for help but something has stolen my voice. I feel trapped. I want to get up and run away from this place, but a gruesome paralysis presses me down.

I see life and death claiming equal parts of my body, ripping it down the middle from head to toe. I struggle hard to stir, but in vain. It's like clapping with one hand. I cannot move my right half an inch without the help of my left half. But my left half is rotting away. The decaying processes of nature are well underway. Flies are swarming over a pile of dirt that used to be my left half.

As I lie here, slipping in and out of consciousness, I realize that this is more than just a terrible nightmare. I ponder the stark simultaneities of life and death, love and hate, peace and war, past and present. Suddenly, history doubles up and sits back on itself like a folded figure-eight. The then/there folds up and merges with the here/now. And it all makes sense. Nightmares do have parallels in waking life.

One long nightmare ended when PEN and Amnesty International secured my release from ten years of imprisonment in Ethiopia, facilitating my arrival in Canada with my three children. But it has now been ten years since I applied to reunite with my husband. For ten years, I have been waiting for an answer.

Canada becomes Ethiopia as history doubles up in this moment of deep reflexivity. And the ten years of imprisonment in Ethiopia fold onto the ten years of my imprisonment in Canada. Yes, I may have run away, but I have not escaped. The torture, fear, waiting, and uncertainty merge in this echoing of history. The compassionate and gracious faces at Immigration Canada simultaneously fold onto its cruelty.

My immediate family is ripped down the middle along gender lines. The female half blossoms while the male half withers away. As I lie here, half alive, half dead, the long history of the African slave comes storming back to the newest African in the free world. The threat of the predator male slave meets the bestiality of the African liberation struggler. The seductive sexuality of the female slave meets the female freedom fighter.

No, bygones are never bygones. They swirl back in endless, vicious cycles. In this reflexive blur, the conscious folds onto the unconscious and the eyes of Immigration Canada merge with the eyes of the slave master. And so ensues my stormy conversation with Immigration Canada.

– – – – –

I spent ten years in a Canadian prison without charge or trial.

Are you sure you mean Canada and not Ethiopia?

Oops! Did I say Canada? A slip of the tongue, I guess. Confusion. A long pensive silence, and then a timid voice comes out of me: sometimes Canada *is* Ethiopia.

I'm not sure you like my translation. But you asked me what *I* meant. I know there is no absolute meaning. I can only tell you what this experience means to me. I can only hold up a mirror and show you what you look like — through the lenses of my own eyes.

I know you don't like it — something told me. Something deep down, or is it something way up there? I look up and see angry clouds gathering on your face, and fear consumes me. Fear of your wrath, of the rage that will rain down on me, of the rumbling thunder that will batter me, of the fuming crater that will open up, of the lava that will engulf my soul. Hold on! I want to swallow my words back.

But why is your question so unsettling? Why is it so disarming and disruptive to my sense of self? I don't know what I'm talking about.

I don't know whether I mean Canada or Ethiopia. I don't know who I am anymore. I'm losing it. I feel dizzy. My heart stops. My knees slip. I fall down on the ground, onto Mother Earth. And I fall down on Akko, my grandmother.

Akko will protect me from your wrath, from your question, from your contagious doubt. You doubt that I said Canada. I doubt it, too. Ethiopia is like a soiled cloth marred with gross human rights violations. It feels so fitting that I spent ten years in its dirty dungeons. But Canada is so clean, so white, so pure. Your doubt is now my doubt — I own it. Ten years without charge or trial? In Canada? That's impossible. Did I really say Canada and not Ethiopia?

Your question is simple and clear and you mean well. The smile on your face is the witness. Oh, how I love it when you smile! Or do I hate it? Which one of your smiles is this now? I can't seem to get it right, but I've had my warnings before. When I see the lion's teeth, I don't mistake it for a smile. Your lion's teeth bite me. They chew me and eat me away. Your juices dissolve me and I pour down — on the ground. I flow into a gentle stream on Mother Earth. I roll into the nooks of Akko's arms. She contains me and sings sweet lullabies to put me to sleep.

Your question shatters me to pieces and my splinters fill the ground. Your brutal gaze batters me into tiny particles of dust, but the dust rises and fills the air. I hang in space like a thick curtain of mist. Light and weightless, airborne and suspended, I dangle in the air — uncertain where the wind might take me next. But Akko is my gravity. She collects the tiniest particles of my dust. She pulls me back and puts me back together. I settle down and hold onto her. She's my anchor — I'm grounded.

Rooted in Akko, rooted in *my* meaning, I'm solid once again. From the safety of her anchor, I can rise and meet you eye to eye. Rooted in her, fear does not consume me. I consume fear. I'm not afraid of your rage. I'm not shaken by your question, your doubt. Take back your fear! It's not mine. Fear belongs to you. Take back your doubt! I refuse to take it. Your doubt belongs to you.

I do mean what I said. To answer your question, I do mean Canada, not Ethiopia. Canada is my newest prison. *You* locked me up for ten years without charge or trial. This is *my* reality. I will not keep quiet and suffer in silence anymore — not after ten years!

You're talking about my Canada! You're calling my Canada a prison. Canada the beacon of freedom! Canada the beacon of hope! Canada the beacon of peace! Canada rescued you, you ungracious devil! Ethiopians were right to throw you in jail after all. You are a serpent who deserves to rot in that Ethiopian prison. You can always go home to your dirty dungeon if you don't like it here. This is my Canada!

This is *my* Canada, too! And I love *my* Canada. This is *my* beacon of hope, too. Indeed it is *my* beacon of home. I was homeless at home and Canada gave me a home. Canada my refuge! Canada my sanctuary! No one defends this sanctuary more passionately than one who has missed it so dearly. I belong to Canada and Canada belongs to me.

I claim membership in this family. I am a citizen of Canada. I *am* Canadian and all my children *are* Canadians. But the soul of my wholeness is plucked and thrown out to wilt. I want my husband here, my children want their father here. But, very sadly, our Canadianness does not guarantee the right to reunite our family. Because of your blind gatekeeping, we do not heal from the wounds Ethiopia continues to inflict on us.

But there is a stark difference between Ethiopian and Canadian prisons. Ethiopia separated our bodies while our souls and spirits remained together. But Canada brings the bodies together and keeps the souls apart. You aim to injure our souls and break our spirits. Now, that's a brutal vicious prison.

You're so obsessed with this metaphor of prison. I hate that! I hope you won't say it again.

Why do you hate that? Have you ever stopped and asked yourself? Would you rather I call it purgatory? A purgatory where I wait for justice. Would that be a better metaphor because I die in the grace of Canadianness? But if it were a purgatory, I would know my sins and pay my penance. This limbo without charge or trial is worse than a purgatory.

By God, you can be so mean!

I'm tired. I'm breaking down. I can't take this any more. I'm leaving.

Good riddance.

No, I'm staying. I won't let you take away my faith in Canada. I won't let you tarnish my profound faith in the goodness in humanity. I won't let you break my spirit. I heard that Nazis tortured people just to find out the breaking point of people's spirits. Is that what you're doing? Are you trying to find out the breaking point of my spirit?

You're killing a fly with a sledgehammer.

But this is not a fly! It's the elephant in the room. And a sledgehammer won't kill it.

You better shut up, woman! All that comes out of your mouth is poison.

You can't stifle me now! I have Akko with me, remember? For ten years, I have been waiting for mercy to come out of your cruel heart. But you've kept me suspended, so I will never settle down and make Canada my home. I live with one foot out of the door, ready to run, wondering when you will throw me out. Which waiting is better? Waiting for the release of my body in Ethiopia or waiting for the release of my soul in Canada?

Now I get it. Oh, poor crybaby. You just can't snap out of your victimhood. You're never grateful whatever we do for you. You were victimized in Ethiopia and we gave you a lot of attention. Now you want that attention again. You know, sometimes victimhood can be very comfortable. You create your own prison in your head. But rather than take responsibility, you point to others and complain. If you want to feel like a victim, well, be my guest!

May the spirit of my ancestors shield me from that! Being your guest means being at war. Who on earth will believe that I am at war with Canada in Canada? This is an invisible war. Whose eyes will be open enough to see the bloodletting in this mansion of peace? Who will believe that there is hell in this paradise?

No, I don't want to be your guest. I ask you to just release my soul. Just do justice and put me back together with my other half.

But he is a violent criminal! You ask me for justice? The only just place for criminals is behind bars.

Violent? Criminal? In whose dictionary? It sounds like you picked up on an Ethiopianist plot. Has it occurred to you that you may be revictimizing the victim? If he is a criminal, charge him. Bring him to justice. Don't let a human being rot in jail without charge or trial. I give you my word to stand by your side and defend my Canada against him. Just don't leave me in the dark because that's what inflicts pain.

In *my* meaning, my other half, just like myself, is a liberation struggler, not a violent criminal. Others committed countless crimes and violence against him, not the other way around. Or perhaps "violent" and "criminal" are your own labels to keep his soul out, because his body is already contaminating the innocent purity of Canada. My other half failed to capture the state, so you receive him with handcuffs. I know how dearly you love and respect criminals who capture the state. You receive them on red carpets. Is there a space between red carpets and handcuffs? Can one just be a common person?

No. There's no "in-between" here. You are either a hero or a villain.

I've heard that before from others. But I thought *you* prided yourself in enjoying the grey areas. This black/white binary is news to me. I wonder how your rejection would shift if my other half were a white man? A millionaire? A female?

Canada is an open society. People come from around the world and from all walks of life. Just look at you. You are not white and you are not a millionaire, but we took you in. We are a compassionate people.

And how I love you for that! I see the goodness in humanity shine through your compassionate face. In that face, you radiate hope and erase my despair. That's why I cannot fathom why you torture my soulmate.

But your soulmate is a terrorist. I loathe terrorists!

Now you give him a new name and loathe the very name you coin. Surely this hate comes from within you and surely it is about you, too. If you turn those eyes inward, you might be surprised to find the culprit there.

You're talking nonsense. You were nice when we took you in.

You like me only when I'm weak and broken, not when I speak up and tell my truth.

You're losing your mind!

You are losing yours!

The men are terrorists. Hunt them down! Women and children are vulnerable. Protect them!

Men! Problem! Men kill! Women! Children! Protect! Women, children, rape!

Hush! You're screaming.

Rape! Scrape! Rape!

Don't scream.

Widow-maker!

Quiet!

Widow-maker!

We're unveiling Afghanistan.

That's a vicious twist! You're unveiling Algeria.

Afghanistan!

Algeria! Can't you see the fighters are women? Men are in jail. It's Algeria. Can't you see Frantz Fanon coming back from the dead? Oh, how history repeats itself and how it repeats itself in unrepeatable ways.

She's messed up. Hold her! Don't lose her; she's still good. Be gentle on her. He is escaping. Hunt him down and catch him. Kill him!

Widow-maker! You're messed up.

Oh, how I hate you!

But I love you.

I love you too, babe.

But I hate you! I hate the way you eye me.

You mean-spirited slut!

Hail the slave master!

Protect the slave women. Protect them from their men.

But the men are in jail.

$-\,-\,-\,-\,-$

After the battering storm, calm descends on the land. Serenity embraces my soul. The storm has washed away all the dust, smog, and haze. Now I can see the world stretching as far and wide as the eye can see. The choking horizon suddenly widens. I sit at the seashore and stare at the sea, stare at Akko.

Akko whispers into my ears and I hear her deep in my bones. I see her pour all the tears of the years into barrels. She fills and seals them one by one. I count ten huge barrels — one for each year of my imprisonment. "Look beyond your little self!" Akko says. She has a way of humbling me. And I see more barrels of tears — hundreds and thousands of them. I am not alone.

I sit in awe and watch Akko as she labours. She turns the barrels into tiny bottles of healing fragrance and hands them over to me. One by one, I throw the bottles into the calm water, like pebbles. The fragile bottle breaks as it hits the sea. Ripples widen and drift apart, leaving the fragrance floating. Some fragments of the bottles take wings and fly away while others take on sails and sail away. A gentle breeze brings the fragrance of healing on the sea to the land.

Almost too late, I realize that I'm throwing parts of Akko each time I throw a bottle. Remorse grips my soul. How can I squander her love so frivolously? I hang onto the last bottle with all the strength I can muster. But Akko sings back to me from the depth of the sea: "You won't get healing unless you give healing!" Tearfully and painfully, I let go of my last bottle.

A very familiar yet strange drama unfolds on the seashore — where the sea and the land gently kiss each other. Sunset and sunrise and night and day float on the same sky at the same time. In this intimate dance of the familiar and the strange, the past and the future, healing and pain, love and hate are intimately woven together.

The sea mirrors the sky. The wails of its mourning intertwine with the sweetness of its melodies. The sea takes away the tears and gives back fragrance. The mourning of the sea and the singing of Akko fill my voice with bittersweet melodies. As I sing I hear my jailer call out after me:

I hear you! I hear you! Now I see what you mean! You have swallowed the cow; don't choke on the tail.

It's only a faint voice from light years away. The ten years of his prison are diminished. It didn't matter whether it was ten years or ten hundred years. The legacy of prisons is much bigger and deeper. Others have laboured before me, but there is work yet to be done. Barrels of tears need to be transformed into bottles of healing fragrance. I pull up my sleeves to join the others and get down to work.

Mehri Yalfani

The Heart's Language

For me, translation looks like emigration from one beloved homeland to another one: living in a new country and assimilating into and accepting a new way of life; uprooting everything familiar to become integrated in a foreign culture. Sometimes, too, translation looks like navigation on a sea one hasn't been charted before or, as Paul Auster writes in *The Book of Illusions*, "Translation is a bit like shovelling coal." At any rate, translation is a captivating ordeal for me. It's said that language is the house of the heart. Whether seen as a change of home, navigating uncharted waters or shovelling coal, one can expect to confront a hard job ahead.

I have experienced translation's ordeal, including, on occasion, people telling me, "You translate your own work, so it won't be hard for you, because you have the freedom to change sentences and write them in a way that allows for more direct translation." To tell the truth, sometimes I do consciously change my own texts to allow for more literal translation but, in so doing, I find my own language loses its flavour and becomes tasteless and bizarre to me. Farsi is a deeply metaphorical language — full of expressions and proverbs that are integrated with literary language — making it very difficult to translate.

When I translated the first collection of my own short stories, I gave it to an English Canadian friend to read and comment upon. When she returned my writing, she had highlighted almost half of each page in bright pink marker. When I saw the degree of editing, I told myself, *Poor stories*, feeling ashamed of my poor English. In fact, it was a humiliation for me. I wanted to submit my work to an English Canadian publisher, with the expectation that it would be accepted for publication and that I would be recognized as a writer in this society.

My friend who is an instructor and teaches English as a second language to newcomers — and who was, in fact, also my landlady at the time — looked at me in a way that a doctor looks at his or her patient and said, "I'm sorry, this is not English. It's too far beyond the English language."

Astounded and mute, I stared at my shameful writing and felt a deep disillusionment. *What should I do, then?* I asked myself.

As she noticed my despairing face, she continued, "I have a suggestion."

I tried to push aside my disappointment, and to be hopeful.

"Everything will be okay," she said, using a phrase I'd heard on many occasions over the previous few years of living in exile, and which had no effect on me. But I pretended to be jubilant and asked her, "What suggestion?" This time, against the harsh reality of my hopes, I really tried to imagine that she was about to show me a magic way to perfect my English and become an expert in literary translation.

She stared at me with her own genuine kindness and sympathy. She said, "If you really want your writing to appear to be written by an English-speaking writer, so it will be publishable here, you should forget your first language and write in English — only English. You should think in English, read English, and speak English."

She saw my stupefied and astounded face, but continued, with even more sternness, "You must know the first language always creates a barrier that interferes with learning the second language. When you are about to speak English, you think first in Farsi and then translate into English. So, your first language is always with you and won't let you get really familiar with English. Everyone who listens to you will recognize quickly that you are speaking a second language."

Offended at her words, I tried to encourage myself by saying, "I don't want anyone to imagine that English is my first language. Obviously, I am Farsi-speaking. Why should I pretend to be English-speaking? Whenever I open my mouth to speak English, it is clear that English is my second language because of my accent. I can't change my accent ..."

She interrupted me, "I know that. You don't need to tell me — I'm an English language instructor. But still, if you want to be a writer with works published in English, as I said, you should forget about your first language ..." and she continued on, giving me the same advice that every language instructor imparts to his or her students.

I didn't want to interrupt her, but her suggestion irritated me. What did she mean? Did I really have to forget my beloved Farsi? Stop speaking, reading, and writing in Farsi? Forget all the poems flowing through me in my own tongue? Is it possible? No, it wasn't possible for me. I couldn't empty myself of my mother language. That was beyond my strength. So I interrupted her, even though I knew I was being rude. "That's impossible," I said, with deep frustration in my heart, "my mother language is my own identity. I can't simply forget it."

She touched my shoulder gently and said, "I'm not saying that you should forget your mother tongue. I'm saying that, when you write in English, forget about Farsi. Try to write directly in English. Train your brain to write in English until you become fluent and proficient in this language. If you translate your own Farsi works, you'll always be considered a translator, and the language of your stories will never be genuine, original."

She mentioned a few writers whose mother tongue wasn't English but whose work, because it was composed directly in English, did not have a problem with language, diction, or expression.

I contested her, "If this or that famous writer writes in English and is successful, he or she might have learned English as a child, either in a home country or in Canada. But for me, it was different. I was middle aged when I immigrated to Canada. English was a subject that I'd taken in high school and college, but my actual knowledge of English was limited to a few simple conversational sentences, such as 'What's your name?' 'How much does it cost?' Or, 'The weather is fine' or 'rainy.' Once in this country, I didn't have the opportunity to go to college to learn English well and make it an internal, metaphorical language for myself. As a writer known well in Iran, I wanted to be recognized in this country as well. I didn't have enough money to pay someone with perfect English to translate my Farsi fiction. So, my only option became to translate my work myself. I'm sure you think it's a huge ambition and a dream beyond my wings' strength. From what you say, it seems I should forget about it."

"You shouldn't give up your dream so quickly," she said. "I've noticed that you're a hard-working writer and that every night your light is on until late."

I felt a cold sweat break out all over my body and a shiver run down my spine. I said to myself, *God help me, she probably wants to increase the rent!* I looked at her with suspicion, suddenly doubting her motives. Perhaps all of her "kind" comments were a fake premise to inform me I was using more electricity than I was allowed.

But, maintaining a soothing tone, she returned to my manuscript, flipping through the pages without paying attention to any particular passage. "I remember one expression that you repeat several times," she said. "'If someone really wants something, they will get it with hard work.' So, you, too, must want it."

I was still disappointed but felt a trace of joy that she hadn't yet mentioned raising the rent. "How?" I asked.

"As I said, forget about your mother language," she said severely, like a teacher instructing her student.

I opened my mouth to say, *I can't, it's impossible*, but she didn't let me utter a word. "Start to think in English, read in English, and write in English. You must do it very seriously and constantly."

As I listened to her, I felt I was navigating waters of a foreign sea. I asked myself, for how long will I be lost on this huge ocean without any shore in sight? And, if after many years of doubting where I would land, what direction would I, could I, take?

My friend, speculating at my lengthy silence and despairing face, asked, "What do you think? What's your idea?"

Like someone standing on the shore at the beginning of this intricate, utterly unknown journey, I said, "I'm afraid to start."

"Why?" she asked, surprised.

"I'm afraid I will reach *nowhere*," I said.

"I can't understand what you mean," she responded flatly.

I said, "It's a Farsi expression and it's very hard to put it into English words exactly as it is."

She laughed loudly and said, "You see, this is the first language's intrigue. You have to release yourself from your first language. You have to forget Farsi expressions and find English expressions with the same concept. If you translate each Farsi expression word for word it will sound ridiculous."

"I can't," I said. "It's not at all an easy task."

"You have to." There was a sense of superiority in her voice.

I stayed quiet, wondering. I felt genuine disappointment. Realizing she could do nothing for me and ready to leave, she repeated once again, "Think about it. If you want to be an English writer, you should write …"

But I didn't hear the rest of her sentence. Too pungent to swallow. I had to find another way, but what would that be? I didn't know.

She placed my writing — which was pinkened all over as though with shame — on the table and thanked me for my hospitality (only black tea, not much) and left. There was still sympathy in her eyes, but now it was tinged with disappointment. Obviously she did not see a bright future for my writing in English. She held her tongue, though, and it was as if my own papers chided me: *Translation isn't an easy job. If you want your works to be published in English, if you want the publisher to get beyond the first few manuscript pages, you must forget your mother language. The sweet rhythmic Farsi that interweaves with and emerges from your flesh and bones. Forget the fairy tales you heard as a child, forget poems from Hafiz, Rumi, Nima Shamloo, Sepehri, Forugh. Leave behind the community newspapers and Iranian websites in which you find beautiful poems to refresh your soul.* All such thoughts made me miserable and on the brink of tears.

I saw my friend beside me, a ghostly voice repeating her pessimistic phrases. "Remember you live in an English-speaking society ..."

I tried to fulfill my friend's recommendation. For a few months I read only English books and newspapers, and wrote in English. I tried, too, to think in English but mostly my mind became blank, as if I had less and less to think about. It seemed as though a murky veil surrounded me, sometimes gloomy, on occasion clear, as if lace curtains separated me from the texts I read.

And when I began to write in English, everything worsened. The words seemed to come, not from my skin and flesh, but from somewhere unknown, where I could neither feel nor touch them. When I wanted to bring a concept to paper, words fled from my memory — disappeared like wisps of smoke in the air, their meanings dissolving in my mind. Even when certain words were part of my general working vocabulary, when I tried to use them in creative writing they seemed to play a game with me, to dash from my mind, leaving me bewildered and frustrated. When I tried to read back my writing, it alienated me, the words ringing without soul or life. They were not my own. Fictional characters were stiff as mannequins, bearing abstract faces and bodies, never more than sketchy armatures for statues I was trying hard to build. I could hardly recognize my own writing. The plot and descriptive passages were foreign to me. A voice inside me yelled, *You're not an English-language writer. Your heart's language is Farsi. Do not make it foreign to yourself. The Farsi, as Jamalzadeh said, is sugar.*

For me, Farsi is indeed even better than sugar, better than anything I can imagine. When I read Rumi's poetry for the first time, in Farsi, my joy was compounded by the realization that I shared this great poet's mother tongue — it could speak directly to my heart.

And, so, again, I took refuge in Farsi. I have chosen to continue to write in my first language and to translate it afterwards, to English. I force myself repeatedly to emigrate from my own beloved land to a foreign one, to wander in its winding alleys and semi-dark hallways. Repeatedly, I attempt to navigate seas on which I find myself afloat for the first time. Each time I emerge into one of these strange and new places, each time I reach a far shore with new earth under my feet, I re-encounter the process of becoming familiar and safe. I know I have a long road ahead of me, a path on which perhaps English will gradually become bright and clear as a language for writing, with the internalized immediacy of my heart's language, my mother tongue.

Goran Simic

Translations of Misunderstandings

As long as I live outside my country of origin, replacing my nest in Sarajevo with one in Toronto, it never becomes clear to me whether exile is a punishment or a reward. As time goes by, I become much more concerned about who's elected mayor of the city I live in than which political party won the last election in Bosnia. Some people call this living in reality instead of clinging to fading memories. Some patriots believe that I was last in line among newly born babies when God was doling out patriotism. None of them are right; I'm not religious at all, and since my writing is mostly based on my past, it seems like the lobotomy on my memory wasn't successful.

On the one hand, every time I pick up an English dictionary searching for the words that will replace the music of the words of my old country, I face a feeling of irreplaceable loss. Thick, heavy, and cold, the dictionary is a book of torture for those who need it. During the siege of Sarajevo, I used dictionaries as blinds for my windows, because they offered the best protection from the incoming bullets. But I never used dictionaries to feed my cold furnace during the winter the way I used magazines or crime novels.

On the other hand, I've believed for the last thirty years — for as long as I've been writing — that my readers are my real countries. So, I shouldn't complain about my audience in Canada. I share with writers born in this language the same worst nightmare: that the readers won't understand what I want to say. I won't go into my private nightmares, where I spend the whole night trying to find the right word to express myself. I am not inclined to share these with anybody who wouldn't understand them.

It took me a long time to realize how my fear of small provincial towns on the margins of importance correlates with my fear of the diminishing importance of the English dictionary. As small towns fight against change, the same thing happens to the language used in everyday life. Since I started learning the language, I've noticed how many people don't listen to each other. They automatically adopt a sort of "condom language" as their protection — protection against conversation as pregnancy, protection against an unexpected consequence. Everyday language, on the other hand, is like a bad habit.

MARKET LANGUAGE

I can't even surprise the cashier at the corner food store, who sees me at least once a day and always treats me the same way; like a good dog you can pet without any fear it will bite you. One morning after she'd repeated her usual communication mantra, "How are you today?" I told her, "Pretty good, I just had a kidney failure," and she said "Good for you." For the next few seconds, I waited for her reaction, to see if a bell would ring in her ear. But she was just waiting for me to pay. I introduced another topic the next time, telling her that my mother couldn't be present at my birth. Her answer was, "Too bad for her," and then she waited a few seconds for me to pay. The same day, after her shift, I met the cashier on the street. This time she was wearing ordinary blue jeans instead of the ugly store clerk's uniform. She asked me the same question, "How are you today?" Then she stopped for a few seconds, as if she were waiting for me to pay.

I've been asking myself if this is a mechanism of plain talk, or talking for the sake of talking, or saying something without saying anything. Is this kind of language applicable only to the capitalist societies, in which spending and spending is desirable? Is the spending of pale words that already have lost their meaning just a consequence of living in a rich society where smiles and spoken words cost nothing? Are words used in the same way as fresh air just because they're free? I'm not talking about highly overpriced lawyer's language, which is a mosaic of rhetoric about which even an average lawyer is unsure. One lawyer told me that if I wanted to decipher the logic of their vocabulary, I should

spend at least $100,000 to finish law school. I didn't want to go that far.
Guessing is cheaper.

Did I practise that kind of "tell me but please don't tell me" language back in Bosnia? I suppose I did. Ten years ago, during the Sarajevo siege, when every conversation was overpowered by noises of grenades and bullets, people at the black market didn't have much time to talk — they were more interested in memorizing your face. The black market was the only place where people could get information about a lost family member or discuss why Bill Clinton was late again in stopping the war. And while they talked, they would stare at you as though you were a conspirator, as though you had a frame around your face. The vendors were mostly older women, and they would caress your hands gently as mothers do, holding the conversation for a few minutes longer. While talking to you they were happy: partly because they were not the only survivors but also because, by memorizing your face, they would recognize it in tomorrow's obituary column and not mistake you for somebody else.

Once, when the price of a battery pack on the black market was on par with the price of gold, I spent almost half an hour trading batteries for cans of meat. While negotiating, I had a chance to learn how to connect dead telephone lines to a transistor radio to make it work. Not to mention receiving advice on how to plant watermelon on my balcony. In the end, calling me a "smart guy," the vendor asked me whether I thought the war would soon be over — a most terrible question. Later on, at home, I wondered who actually was the smart guy: the person who exchanged the battery pack for just three cans of meat or the vendor, who would get six cans for the pack. But at least I received the vendor's attention for half an hour, and that was priceless.

Was it worth paying a double price for being noticed? Yes. While talking with that old lady I could have been killed or she could have been arrested by the black market mob. But while we were talking, our language had a human face.

POETRY LANGUAGE

Some years ago, after my book launch in Amsterdam, I had a short and heated conversation with one of the directors of the famous Amsterdam Literary Festival. As a new Canadian, I casually asked him why there were so few Canadian poets on the list of festival guests. He answered honestly, telling me that they had tried some years ago. What made me contemplate the status of Canadian poetry was his remark that they had once invited some Canadian poet. This person read in front of the fully packed theatre, and nobody in the audience could tell when the poet's introduction to the poem stopped and when the poetry reading started.

Empty words again, plus empty words on the stage. I disagreed with him, trying to persuade him to read the beautiful poems by A.F. Moritz, Patrick Lane, Alden Nowlan, and Ken Babstock. Unfortunately, the festival director was already focused on somebody who was promoting the beauty of new Bulgarian poetry.

This experience was enough to lead me to the poetry section at the Toronto Reference Library, my temporary home and almost native land. After two months of visiting the deserted poetry section on the second floor, one day I noticed a young woman sitting in my favourite chair with a poetry book. My first thought was that she must be hiding from somebody. Usually people hide in the places nobody visits, and unfortunately in Toronto, this happens to be a library poetry section. But to be honest, I was happy to have somebody sitting in my chair, somebody who was reading Al Purdy's selected poems. And I told her the story of how Fraser Sutherland introduced me to Purdy. Purdy asked me if I had come to Canada to become its best poet. I said of course I did — who would come to Canada to be the second-best poet? Purdy informed me that I'd only have a chance at that position after he died. He died the next year, and after that, I didn't have the same ambitions.

Before I even finished telling my Al Purdy story, the young lady, who seemed to have been listening, abruptly told me, "Have a nice day," turning her head the other way. I didn't need a dictionary for that. Seeing myself reflected in her eyes and thinking that I must look like an old pervert to her, I started laughing. I was laughing at myself; someone who had been seduced by the beauty of English literature. A long time ago, I promised myself that I would not learn English. I didn't want to spoil my native language. Now, ten years later, I find myself not only speaking English, but even trying to drag a Canadian into Canadian poetry.

I had a similar experience when I got my first laptop computer and fell in love with that little brain packed in a plastic body. Before I got my first computer, I was against that kind of technology, believing it diminished the imagination. Later on, I found myself discussing the beauty of the computer with my children. But I was too late. They already knew more than I did. People change.

The young woman got a hostile expression on her face when I began to laugh, and she swore at me as she left. For that, once again, I didn't need a dictionary. Was Al Purdy such a maniac, I wondered, and I picked up the book she was reading to check what was in it, to understand why an already dead poet had upset her so much. Under the book I found a scrap of paper with a note from somebody named Jim. The note, addressed to "Jane", read "See you in the poetry section at the Toronto Reference Library at 2:30 PM. Love you so much, Jim."

I would have felt guilty bribing that young girl with poetry if I hadn't noticed that she had crossed out the name on the top of Jim's letter and written in a nervous scribble, "My name is Julia, idiot."

I didn't need a dictionary to understand the language of disappointment. And I was happy, at last, to see that language does have universal meaning.

Some time later, I completed an anthology of Canadian poetry and translated it with my wife, Visnja, into the language people once called Serbo-Croatian. This language doesn't officially exist. Yugoslavia, where I was born, doesn't exist anymore either. But the people from that dead country, divided by frontiers, and to whom I dedicated the beauty of poetry, still communicate using that dead language. From either side of these new frontiers, we have lived the same horror with a different meaning. At least we don't rely on a dictionary to read poets writing from thousands of miles away.

MISTRANSLATIONS

The other night I was trying to make a list of times in my life when I was erroneously translated. Or misunderstood. I excluded poetry from that list after I learned that some of my poems had been translated from Serbo-Croatian into Italian, and from Italian into Bulgarian. I suppose I don't live in those translations at all. I'm thinking about situations when simple details are perceived differently, just because of different eyes and ears.

Life would be very dull if we all used the same dictionary. Where would art be if everything was clear? As a writer, I never liked to wear a uniform. If somebody invented eyeglasses that allowed one to see everything clearly, I'd be the first one to lose them on purpose. There might be less confusion and pain in life, but it would be a boring life.

I still believe in the old adage: If you hit the target, you will miss everything around the target.

I would have been close to finishing my life list of mistranslations one night while sitting on my porch, if the raccoons hadn't come every few minutes to check if I was sleeping. Or, if the morning hadn't come so suddenly to find out why I was crying. Here is my partial list that anybody can read without a dictionary.

THE BOY AND MY PICTURE BOOK

In the middle of the Sarajevo siege I was running along a street to get home before the curfew, and just before I reached my doorway I bumped into a little six-year-old boy. The city was full of refugees from burned villages who had come with horror stories. It didn't take me long to realize by looking at his dirty clothes that he came from nowhere, as did so many kids roaming the city. But I stopped because under his arm he was holding the only children's picture book that I'd ever written. It was published a long time before the war, and it happened to be the only one of my books I didn't possess because I'd given all my copies away to kids.

"Would you give me that book in exchange for the chocolate?" I tempted that six-year-old boy; having in my pocket two chocolates that my friends had sent for my children.

"No way," he told me, and stepped back, holding his book tighter.

"What about two chocolate bars for that book?" I tried to negotiate, looking around to see if the curfew police were nearby. They'd already arrested me once, telling me to consider myself lucky because they didn't shoot me.

"No way," he told me in a harsh voice. "Every night I read this picture book to my little sister and, by the way, why do you need this book?"

"Because I am the author," I told him, taking two chocolate bars out of my pocket, ready to give them to him as a present. I would never tell my children about those chocolate bars.

"If you are the author, you don't need this book because you know what it's about," and he quickly started running towards the end of the street.

I found myself running after him. I wanted to tell him that I didn't need that book — it was written at a happy time. I wanted to tell him the war would be over soon and that his parents would be back. I just wanted to tell him that he could bring his sister over and play with my children. But I was shouting that I'd give him two chocolate bars for free.

The boy didn't hear me; he kept running towards the end of the street, screaming that he didn't want the chocolate. At the corner of the street, I saw him bump into heavily armed curfew police, and then he ran away into the night.

I left the two chocolate bars on the pavement and went upstairs to my two children, who'd already been woken up by the noise on the street. I didn't tell them anything about the chocolate bars. There is no language or dictionary to help explain what happened.

The next morning my son went downstairs to play. A few minutes later, he came back excited, with two chocolate bars he'd just found on the pavement.

If the little boy survived the war, and I hope he did, I suppose he would be around seventeen years old — just like my son. I still don't have that picture book and my fingers are still sticky from those chocolate bars.

SUSAN AND THE TWO SUITCASES

When Susan found a way to get into besieged Sarajevo for the first time, she brought us bags full of food. We placed the food on the table so we could look at it all day long, enjoying the scene of a full table. Susan told me that she could understand the beauty of watching.

When she was leaving for New York, we asked Susan to take some of our photos with her, to keep them safe in case we survived. I gave her my old suitcase packed with our past.

The next time Susan came, the suitcase was packed with presents. I unpacked the presents and placed the empty suitcase on the table. For the next few hours, we watched it, scarcely paying attention to the food on the floor.

Susan didn't understand our passionate glances at the empty suitcase. Actually, we were admiring the travel stickers: New York, Berlin, Vienna ... what food for the eyes of prisoners.

TRANSISTOR RADIO

I was never so ashamed of myself as in the summer of 1995. I found myself lying on a quiet Italian beach, playing with my children in the sand, far from the snipers and the besieged city — far from danger. Suddenly, upset by trying in vain to find a Bosnian radio station with news of the war, I threw my little transistor radio into the sea.

No more news means no more bad news, I told myself. I turned my attention to the drawings my children were doing in the sand. My daughter had just made a picture of a butterfly and my son was struggling to shape a bird.

Suddenly, a little wet gypsy boy appeared, holding my soaked and discarded transistor radio in his hand. Everything would be okay, he told me, if I let it dry and bought new batteries. I watched the little guy, who was already running back to the sea, and I wanted to ask him how many transistor radios he'd already saved from the depths. I wanted to hear that I was not the only sad man who wondered: who am I to be a survivor?

How many others had thrown their transistor radios into the sea, only to secretly go to the shop to buy new batteries, as I did?

But the boy was already gone and I couldn't remember the language he had spoken. The only traces of him were his footprints in the sand on my daughter's butterfly and my son's bird.

Biographies

Contributors

ZDENKA ACIN was one of the most prominent print and broadcast journalists in the former Yugoslavia before she came to Canada in 1999. One of her several published books is a collection of essay-interviews on international dissident authors (Czeslaw Milosz, Joseph Brodsky, and Josef Skvorecky, among others). She is now living in Toronto.

REZA BARAHENI was born in Tabriz, Iran, in 1935. He is the author of fifty-four books, including *The Crowned Cannibals*, a collection of prose and poetry, and *Les Saisons en Enfer du Jeune Ayyaz*, a novel. His *God's Shadow: Prison Poems* is a collection of poems based on a period of 102 days spent in solitary confinement in Iran, during the time of the Shah. He was also imprisoned in the fall of 1981 and the winter of 1982 by the Islamic Republic of Iran. He is one of two scholars to join the new Scholars-at-Risk Program at U of T's Massey College and is presently a visiting professor at the university's Centre for Comparative Literature.

ANDREA HILA is a journalist and writer from Shkodra, Albania, who immigrated to Canada in 2002. From 1993 to 2003, he was a correspondent in northern Albania for international German radio Deutsche Welle. He has also been a humanitarian aid worker. As a literary writer, Andrea Hila has published, in 1994, a collection of poetry and, in 1996, a book of short stories, which was awarded the 1997 prize for best first book of prose by the Albanian Ministry of Culture. He now lives in Toronto.

MARTHA KUMSA was born in Oromo and raised in Ethiopia. She worked as a journalist in the latter half of the 1970s in Ethiopia and was incarcerated without charge or trial for ten years (1980–1989). She was released when Amnesty International, PEN International, and PEN Canada launched a successful campaign on her behalf. She was brought to Canada in 1991 with her three children. Her husband joined the family in 1996. Their children are all university graduates now. Kumsa recently completed her PhD and is teaching at Wilfrid Laurier University, while her husband has just published his second book. Their eldest daughter is now a mother, making them proud grandparents.

STELLA LEE lives with her daughter in Toronto, where she is building a new life and working to free her husband, Chinese journalist Jiang Weiping.

FERESHTEH MOLAVI was born in Tehran and worked there as a freelance editor and translator, as well as a librarian and scholar. She has published a novel (*The House of Cloud and the Wind*), a collection of short stories (*The Sunny Fairy*), and two prose works (*The Orange and the Lime, The Iranian Garden*). She has also compiled and published a comprehensive bibliography of short stories in Persian or translated into Persian. In 1998 she came to Toronto and since then has published some stories and articles in Toronto Iranian magazines *Shahrvand* and *Sepidar*, and a literary online website, Sokhan. She has also published a collaborative chapbook, with Canadian writer Karen Connelly, under the auspices of PEN Canada. Molavi is currently living in New Haven, and working with Yale University to develop a Persian collection for the Sterling Memorial Library.

FARUK MYRTAJ was born in a small mining town in Albania. Since his first book in 1985, he has published poetry, short stories, novels, essays, and translations, including translations of a number of Canadian authors. One of his books won the award for the best book of short stories for 1996, given by the Albanian Ministry of Culture. He has also worked as a journalist. Myrtaj came to Canada with his family in 1993.

SENTHILNATHAN RATNASABAPATHY is a journalist from Sri Lanka. He was born in Central Sri Lanka, but grew up in the capital, Colombo, in West Sri Lanka. In 1983, he became a refugee (an "internally displaced person") and moved to North Jaffna. In order to make a living he left high school and in 1985 became a trainee at the premier Tamil daily newspaper in North Sri Lanka, learning the profession amidst falling shells and bombs, and killings. He moved to the capital in 1987 after the Indian military launched operations in the North, and managed to smuggle the first photo out of the area, which was published in *Time* magazine. He lost his job in early 1988 when the Tamil rebels bombed the paper's head office. He then moved to English journalism and freelanced for, among others, the Inter Press Service (IPS) news agency. He forayed into the war territory in the North and East and wrote a number of articles. As a Tamil, he had unique insights into the mindset of the civilians, but that landed him in trouble as some of his interviewees were threatened. He left Sri Lanka in 1990 as a refugee and as an exile, after the Chief Correspondent for the IPS was kidnapped and murdered, and he himself felt threatened. Until 1999, he lived in Vienna and worked as a freelance journalist. He immigrated to Canada in 1999. Currently, he works freelance as the Associate Producer for the Tamil Programme of OMNI.2 TV, and is also the chief editor of a Tamil quarterly, *Ulakathamiloosai*. He is also editor of Shanthi, an online journal promoting peace and understanding in Sri Lanka.

BENJAMÍN SANTAMARÍA OCHOA is a writer, journalist, actor, and teacher from Mexico, who came to Canada in 2002. He has published two books for young adults in Mexico. In 1997, he was appointed as Mexico's first Children's Ombudsman (a post which eventually led to his arrival in Canada as a convention refugee, after his lawyer was murdered). Santamaría is working on a youth novel called *The Monkey-King*, contracted for publication in Canada with Tundra Books. He is currently living in Wolfville, Nova Scotia and holding a one-year writer's residency at Acadia University.

GEORGE BWANIKA SEREMBA was born in Kampala, Uganda and went to Makerere University, Kampala. He was forced to leave Uganda in 1980, having barely survived a botched execution at the hands of military intelligence, and then moved to neighbouring Kenya where he wrote a number of poems and wrote and directed several one-act plays. His first full-length play was entitled *The Grave Will Decide*, and was written in Winnipeg during his first year in Canada. His play *Come Good Rain* debuted at Toronto's Factory Theatre Studio Café, and has also played in Ottawa, Montreal, Los Angeles, London (England), Jerusalem, and elsewhere. Seremba also won a Dora Award for Most Outstanding New Play. Versions of the play were also broadcast on CBC and BBC radio. His most recent play, *Napoleon of the Nile*, has had a number of professional readings. He recently earned an M.Phil. in Irish Theatre and Film Studies from Trinity College, Dublin.

GORAN SIMIC is a Bosnian writer who came to Toronto in 1995 under PEN Canada's sponsorship. Goran has published more than ten books of poetry, drama and short fiction, and his work has been translated into nine different languages. Last year he published his first book in Canada, a collection of poetry titled *Immigrant Blues* (Brick Books); two more books, a collection of new stories titled *Yesterday's People*, and a reissue of his poetry collection *Sarajevo Sorrow* will be published this year by Biblioasis.

MEHRI YELFANI was born in Hamadan, Iran. She published her first book of stories in 1966, then a novel in 1980. She came to Canada in 1985, and since then has published two collections of short stories and three novels, written in Farsi. Two of her story collections, *Parastoo* and *Two Sisters*, have been translated into English and published in Canada by Women's Press and TSAR Press; a novel, *Afsaneh's Moon*, was published by McGilligan Books in 2002. She is currently working on the translation of her first two novels.

Editors

DR. STEPHEN AHERN teaches in the Department of English and runs the Writing Centre at Acadia University. He specializes in teaching writing skills, as well as 18th- and 19th-century British literature.

MARGARET CHRISTAKOS is a Toronto poet and novelist who co-ordinated the Readers and Writers programme at PEN Canada, which assists writers living in exile in Canada.

KAREN CONNELLY is an award-winning poet, essayist, and novelist who divides her time between Toronto and warmer places.

ALAN CUMYN is the author of eight novels, including *The Sojourn* and *Burridge Unbound*. He lives in Ottawa and is chair of the Writers in Prison Committee of PEN Canada.

JANICE KULYK KEEFER lives in Toronto, teaches at the University of Guelph, and has published books of poetry, memoir, literary criticism, and fiction, of which the latest is the novel *Thieves.*

KEN SIMONS is the managing editor of *Peace Magazine* in Toronto.

FRASER SUTHERLAND is a writer and lexicographer who lives in Toronto.

ELKE WILLMAN works in the Department of Languages and Literature at Acadia University.

Coordinating Editor

MAGGIE HELWIG has published books of poetry, essays, and fiction, most recently the novel, *Between Mountains*. She has edited anthologies of short fiction, and worked for human rights groups including the East Timor Alert Network and War Resisters' International. She lives in Toronto and is a member of PEN Canada's Writers in Exile Committee.